Business as Ministry

A Theological, Missiological, and Managerial Integration

Setting Sail for The Common Good

Eric Z.M. Ma, DIS, MBA

BUSINESS AS MINISTRY SERIES

Volume 1
Business as Ministry
A Theological, Missiological, and Managerial Integration

Volume 2
Shaping a Godly Business
A BaM Monday Companion

Volume 3
Godly Business Formation
A BaM Workbook

Volume 4
ServantShip
A BaM PrayBook

Business as Ministry
A Theological, Missiological, and Managerial Integration
Setting Sail for The Common Good.

© 2025 by CGT Research Institute, LLC
All rights reserved.

No part of this book may be reproduced, stored in a retrieval system, or transmitted in any form or by any means—electronic, mechanical, photocopying, recording, scanning, or otherwise—without written permission from the publisher, except as permitted under Sections 107 or 108 of the U.S. Copyright Act.

Published by CGT Research Institute, LLC
Newark, Delaware, U.S.A.
www.cgt-ri.com
Printed in the United States of America

ISBN 979-8-9943932-0-8

Library of Congress Control Number: 2026901564

Cover design: Eric Z.M. Ma
Interior design and layout: Eric Z.M. Ma
Illustrations: Eric Z.M. Ma

Scripture quotations are taken from *The Holy Bible, New International Version®, NIV®.*
Copyright © 1973, 1978, 1984, 2011 by Biblica, Inc.™ Used by permission. All rights reserved worldwide.

For permissions, requests, or information about products and services, please contact:
cgt@cgt-ri.com
www.cgt-ri.com

PUBLISHER'S NOTE

This book is designed to offer perspectives and reflections for individuals and organizations pursuing business as ministry. It is not intended as legal, financial, or management advice. Readers should consult professional advisors for specific applications.

TABLE OF CONTENTS

LIST OF TABLES AND FIGURES	ix
FOREWORD	x
ABBREVIATIONS	xiv
ACKNOWLEDGEMENTS	xviii
ABOUT THIS BOOK SERIES	xx
ABOUT THIS INTEGRATIO	xxii
PREFACE	xxiv
INTRODUCTION	xxvii

1. FOUR PHILOSOPHIES IN BUSINESS   3

1.1 The Law of the Jungle	3
1.2 The Law of Exchange	5
1.3 The Law of Moral Sentiments	6
1.4 The Law of Gratuitousness	8

2. FOUR MODELS IN BUSINESS   13

2.1 The Shareholder Wealth Maximization Model	13
2.2 The Stakeholder Theory Model	17
2.3 The Common Good Model	20
2.4 The Business as Ministry Model	23

3. A 4×4 MATRIX IN BUSINESS   29

3.1 The 4×4 Matrix	29
3.2 The Business Ocean	33
3.3 The Implication of the 4×4 Matrix	35
3.4 The Application of the 4×4 Matrix	36

4. FROM DISCERNMENT TO MEASUREMENT 41

4.1 Research Design 41

4.2 Why Constructivist Worldview, Qualitative Method, and Inductive Approach 42

4.3 Field Procedures, Data, and Analysis 43

4.4 Main Results and Implications 44

5. THE COMMON GOOD TREASURE 49

5.1 The Common Good Treasure 49

5.2 Spiritual Capital — Rudder 50

5.3 Social Capital — Adhesive 53

5.4 Intellectual Capital — Engine 55

5.5 Financial Capital — Fuel 57

5.6 The Vessel in Motion 59

6. MEASURING THE COMMON GOOD TREASURE 63

6.1 From Concept to Measurement 63

6.2 Why We Need the CGTA 64

6.3 The CGTA Framework 65

6.4 The CGTA Items and Scoring 67

6.5 Interpreting Your CGTA Profile 71

6.6 Using CGTA for Growth 75

6.7 From Score to Transformation 76

7. FROM SCHOLARSHIP TO PRACTICE 79

7.1 Using an analogy 79

7.2 Reading the weather 80

7.3 Reading the geology   81
7.4 The ocean and its seas   82
7.5 Reading the treasure with a chart   83
7.6 The Journey of Volume 1   84
7.7 The Framework of Volumes 1, 2, 3, and 4   86

REFERENCES   88

APPENDICES   92
APPENDIX A. GLOSSARY OF KEY TERMS   92
APPENDIX B. SCRIPTURE INDEX AND THEOLOGICAL NOTES   93
APPENDIX C. CGTA TECHNICAL MANUAL   94
APPENDIX D. CGTA INSTRUMENTS   95
APPENDIX E. CASE STUDIES   96
APPENDIX F. PERMISSIONS, DATA AVAILABILITY, AND PLATE CREDITS   102

LIST OF TABLES AND FIGURES

Table 1. CGTA	68
Table 2. Scripture Index and Theological Notes	93
Figure 1. The Framework of Volumes 1, 2, 3, and 4	xxi
Figure 2. Volume 1 Framework	xxiii
Figure 3. The Fundamental Capital Flow Map	14
Figure 4. SWM Capital Flow Map	16
Figure 5. ST Capital Flow Map	18
Figure 6. CG Capital Flow Map	22
Figure 7. BaM Capital Flow Map	24
Figure 8. The 4×4 Matrix color semantics	30
Figure 9. The 4 Quadrants of the 4×4 Matrix color semantics	34
Figure 10. The Common Good Treasure - CGT	66
Figure 11. The Vessel – CGTA	67
Figure 12. CGTA Radar Chart	70
Figure 13. Balanced Vessel with Kingdom-Flourishing Alignment	71
Figure 14. Leaning Vessel with Profitable Drift	72
Figure 15. Leaking Vessel with Righteous Stagnation	73
Figure 16. Underdeveloped Vessel as a Beginner	74
Figure 17. The journey of Volume 1	85
Figure 18. The framework of Volumes 1, 2, 3, and 4	87
Figure 19. The CGT Movement of the Agricultural Enterprise	97
Figure 20. The Movement of the Agricultural Enterprise on the 4x4 Matrix	97
Figure 21. The CGT Movement of the Health Informatics	99
Figure 22. The Movement of the Health Informatics on the 4x4 Matrix	99
Figure 23. The CGT Movement of the Textile Manufacturer	101
Figure 24. The Movement of the Textile Manufacturer on the 4x4 Matrix	101

FOREWORD

As an academic scholar who loves research, I usually read research with an eye to see the practical and theoretical significance or implications of the research findings. Some researchers excel at envisioning how their research findings could be practically useful in their field. Eric Ma is one of the researchers who saw the profound implications of his field research and took the initiative to create instruction and instruments that would benefit the field of Business as Ministry (BaM). This book, Business as Ministry, represents his efforts to communicate the underlying framework for his evolving understanding and proposed instruments to aid businesses moving toward models that holistically express the love of God and the love for neighbors in ways that demonstrate Kingdom of God values within and outside the business. In Volume 1, Eric Ma first describes four philosophies of business that frame discussions of business models and help to understand diverse business models. I personally found Eric Ma's discussion of four models in business and the associated graphics very helpful in describing components of business, and his insights into their connections and influence on business direction and outcomes very insightful. By way of describing each model, Eric Ma leads the reader down the path of discovering differentiations of connections, influences, and implications that distinctly matter in efforts to create Godly businesses.

I met Eric Ma at the early stages of his research planning when he was still exploring the literature related to BaM, wrestling with the theological and missiological bases of business, and exploring various models of business, including the Common Good Model. I continued to walk with him through his on-the-ground observations and interviews with real-life businesses working for the common good. In this volume, Eric Ma takes the reader beyond his analysis and description of four business models to present research evidence of firms in the field attempting to demonstrate the love of God and love for neighbors and community through their conceptions of business as ministry. Eric Ma incorporates stories from these and other businesses to flesh out the four kinds of capital described by businesspeople running businesses as Christian ministries. He continues to elaborate on the evolving concepts of the Common Good Treasure, using an extensive metaphor of BaM as a vessel navigating God's Ocean and laying out extensive assessment tools based on the Common Good Treasure. Eric Ma's Volume 1 is rich not only in theoretical understanding and concrete narrative evidence but also in well-thought-out instruments that can be used by businesspeople who seriously want to begin exploring their own business through the Business as Ministry Model, the 4x4 Matrix, and the Common Good Treasure Assessment instrument. This volume of work springs out of extensive observations and interviews with businesspeople whose hearts are set on journeying into the unchartered world of business as ministry. This makes Eric Ma's research findings a significant contribution to anyone who is considering launching into the world of business as ministry and to those who may have already launched out on the journey but want to better understand and improve how to navigate that world.

Jane Rhoades, PhD
Dissertation Supervisor
Talbot Theological Seminary, Biola University
Former Trainer and Teacher in Africa

FOREWORD

Dr. Eric Z.M. Ma's "*Business as Ministry*" delights with intellectuality and surprises with practicality. As a seasoned practitioner and having digested a small library of business books over my lifetime, I did not expect this academic volume to be so fresh and useful.

Dr. Ma's work will energize any enterprise whose owners have spiritual aspirations by crafting a lens through which to observe key dimensions of success over time and a language to talk about them. New measurements allow for better management.

Beyond that, it promises to stimulate further academic inquiry in the field by merging theology, missiology, and organizational theory into a conceptual framework that others can build on. It integrates the "why" and "what" of a profitable business as a Christian ministry, challenging stereotypes of "spiritual" and "secular" values.

Much has been written previously about "multiple bottom line" business and the recognition of trade-offs between apples and oranges. What is new with this book is a tool for stakeholders to visualize and balance these tradeoffs over time, then seek consensus on what actions to take next.

This result is due to Dr. Ma's resume as much as his research. Before beginning doctoral studies, he founded companies, consulted on nuclear power plant construction, and became a hydroponics expert. In other seasons, he served in humanitarian causes, like disaster recovery operations in Fukushima, and missions (schools and churches) in Uganda.

His graduate studies include a master's degree from Fuller Theological Seminary and a doctorate from Biola University, based on research he conducted in America's rural Midwest. "The

Common Good Treasure," his commonsense framework, encompasses four types of capital that interact with each other. Stewardship of God's creation (people and planet) is measured alongside traditional financial measures of business performance. His assessment method distills useful metrics despite the inherent imprecision of such soft measures, making a possible better understanding of tradeoffs and clearer discussions of them.

I trust you will find the book well organized, presenting a brief survey of the literature and grounding the Common Good Treasure model in both theory and case studies. You will also benefit from his preview of Volumes 2, 3, and 4 of this series, which are written for practitioners who are putting the model to use in strategic decision-making.

The book never loses sight of the fact that businesses must stay focused on their core functions, but it also emphasizes their calling in Christ to be more than just efficient machines. It takes neither a romantic nor a cynical view of business; instead, it offers a well-reasoned, empirically based, and optimistic perspective on how profitable businesses can contribute to God's mission.

Paul Condrell
Former Founder and Chairman
Healthy Household Limited and The Fountains Community Center
Guangzhou, China

ABBREVIATIONS

GENERAL ABBREVIATIONS

BaM	Business as Ministry
BAM	Business as Mission
CG	Common Good
CGT	Common Good Treasure
CGTA	Common Good Treasure Assessment
CSR	Corporate Social Responsibility
EPS	Earnings per Share
FI	Financial (capital)
IN	Intellectual (capital)
IP	Intellectual Property
IRB	Institutional Review Board
LOP	Lausanne Occasional Paper
NIV	New International Version Bible (2011)
NPV	Net Present Value
OKR	Objectives and Key Results
PII	Personally Identifiable Information
RAEF	Rudder · Adhesive · Engine · Fuel
R&D	Research & Development
ROI	Return on Investment
SO	Social (capital)
SOP	Standard Operating Procedure(s)
SP	Spiritual (capital)
ST	Stakeholder Theory
SWM	Shareholder Wealth Maximization
U.S.	United States
WACC	Weighted Average Cost of Capital

BIBLICAL BOOKS ABBREVIATIONS

Gen.	Genesis
Exod.	Exodus
Deut.	Deuteronomy
Ps.	Psalms
Prov.	Proverbs
Mic.	Micah
Matt.	Matthew
Rom.	Romans
1 Cor.	1 Corinthians
2 Cor.	2 Corinthians
Gal.	Galatians
Eph.	Ephesians
Col.	Colossians
1 Thess.	1 Thessalonians
Rev.	Revelation

"Whatever you do, do it all for the glory of God."

—1 Corinthians 10:31b, New International Version Bible

To every scholar and practitioner alike in the field of business as ministry,
who works diligently
to honor God through lecturing, writing, and practicing,
and to quietly do good even when unseen.
You embody the truth that the gospel can flourish
in research and development.
May this book inspire you to align your
wisdom,
creativity,
insight, and
knowledge, to
transform your scholarship into
a vessel of God's goodness—The Common Good.

ACKNOWLEDGEMENTS

I offer my deepest gratitude to our Almighty God for His unwavering mercy and divine guidance throughout this inspiring journey of writing. The Spirit has provided me with strength every step of the way, enveloped me in grace, and illuminated my path with wisdom. This book series is a testament to Jesus' unconditional love and abundant blessings.

I extend my earnest appreciation to the research institutes where my journey of scholarship has left its mark.

Biola University
Fuller Theological Seminary
California State University, East Bay
University of California, Berkeley

These institutions embody God's wisdom, inspiration, and encouragement. They stand as beacons of light in the realm of knowledge. Their continuous support has been a source of strength, and I am deeply appreciative of my peers' enthusiasm for my research and their insightful critiques, which have refined my ideas. This book series is a testament to academic rigor and my personal transformation, nurtured by these institutions' steadfast commitment to education as a mission for the common good.

To Mabel, my beloved wife and companion, and Derron, my treasured son and friend, from whom love blossomed and aspirations soared. Every page of this book echoes your names, for your unwavering belief in me has shaped this scholarship zenith. Your steadfast faith illuminated my journey, your quiet prayers anchored my resolve, and your infinite love was the unswerving impetus behind my ascent to this summit.

Thank you to all the entrepreneurs, managers, employees, and community leaders who shared their stories graciously. Your integrity has shown me that credible companies can reflect the Kingdom. To the peer readers and editors who pushed for clarity—thank you for enhancing the arguments and practicality of this work.
For churches and small groups that hosted workshops, you transformed this solitary project into a community effort. Thank you, friends, for reminding me to take breaks. Your support, both emotional and financial, is woven throughout this manuscript.

Finally, to the readers: Thank you for your trust! My prayer is that the following pages guide you toward the Common Good Treasure, balancing spiritual devotion with practical stewardship and ultimately serving Christ and the community.

May the work of our hands be established (Psalm 90:17, NIV).

Soli Deo Gloria.

Eric Z.M. Ma
Newark, Delaware, U.S.A.

ABOUT THIS BOOK SERIES

This four-volume series, "Business as Ministry," is designed as a cohesive journey that integrates theology, research, practice, and formation.

Volume 1 – Business as Ministry: A Theological, Missiological, and Managerial Integration
This volume lays a scholarly foundation by integrating biblical theology, missiology, and management. It presents key frameworks, including the 4×4 "ocean" matrix, the Common Good Treasure (CGT), and the Common Good Treasure Assessment (CGTA).

Volume 2 – Shaping a Godly Business: A BaM Monday Companion
This volume translates these insights into a practical guide, offering weekly disciplines, operational practices, and governance tools for leaders and teams.

Volume 3 – Godly Business Formation: A BaM Workbook
This volume serves as a workbook with guided exercises, case studies, and group processes, enabling individuals, organizations, and learning communities to embody the principles of Business as Ministry over time.

Volume 4 – ServantShip: A BaM PrayBook
This volume is a devotional prayerbook for spiritual formation in business. It invites leaders and teams to devote their work to God through Scripture, prayer, confession, and worship—anchoring everything in a posture of shalom as the vessel arrives at its deepest calling.

Figure 1, "The Framework of Volumes 1, 2, 3, and 4," visually places each book within the overarching journey, showing how scholarly integration, practical tools, formative exercises, and devotional practice converge in one calling.

Figure 1. The Framework of Volumes 1, 2, 3, and 4

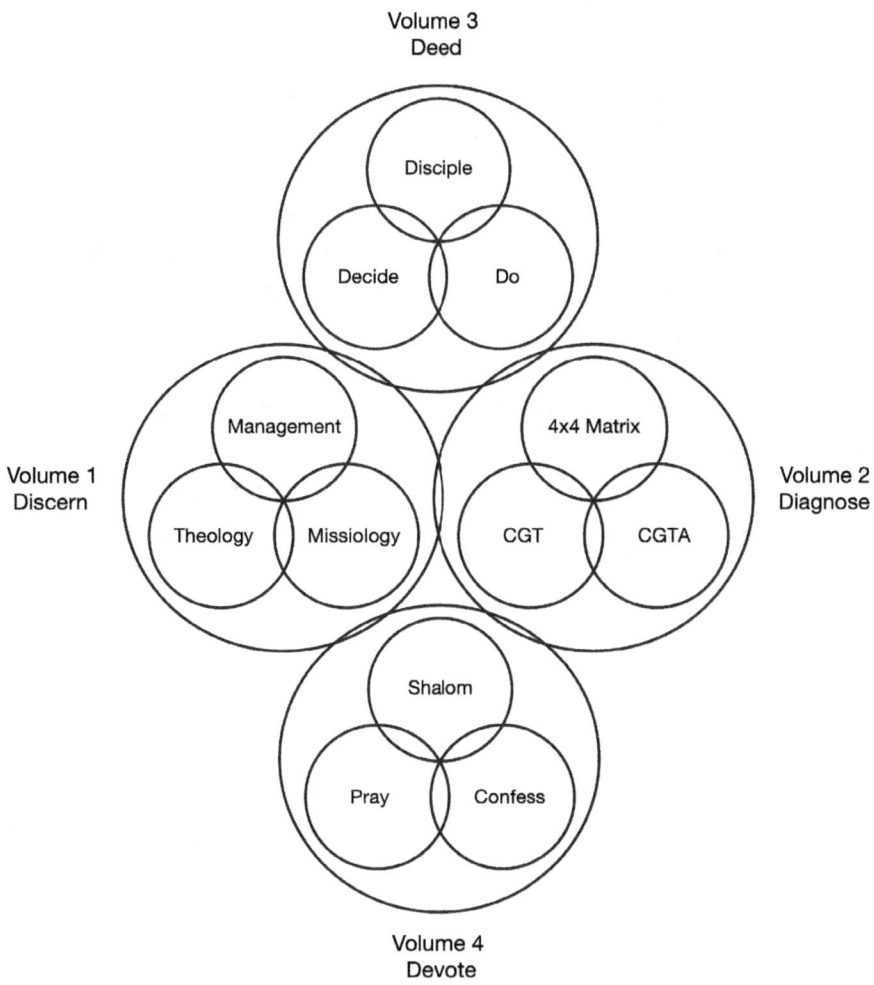

ABOUT THIS INTEGRATION

Volume 1 traces the integration of theology, missiology, and business management into a coherent research narrative. It begins with biblical and theological discernment of the common good and examines four business philosophies. The discussion then moves on to various business models, culminating in a 4×4 matrix presented as an "ocean." It then transitions to the field through qualitative inquiry, focusing on real companies in their specific contexts.

From this practical exploration, the Common Good Treasure (CGT) and the Common Good Treasure Assessment (CGTA) are developed as a constructive framework for both scholarly pursuits and organizational development.

Figure 1, "*Volume 1 Framework*," visually maps this progression. It moves from foundational questions to empirical study, measurement, and interpretation, forming a unified arc of scholarly integration that sets the stage for the more practice-oriented Volumes 2, 3, and 4.

Figure 2. Volume 1 Framework

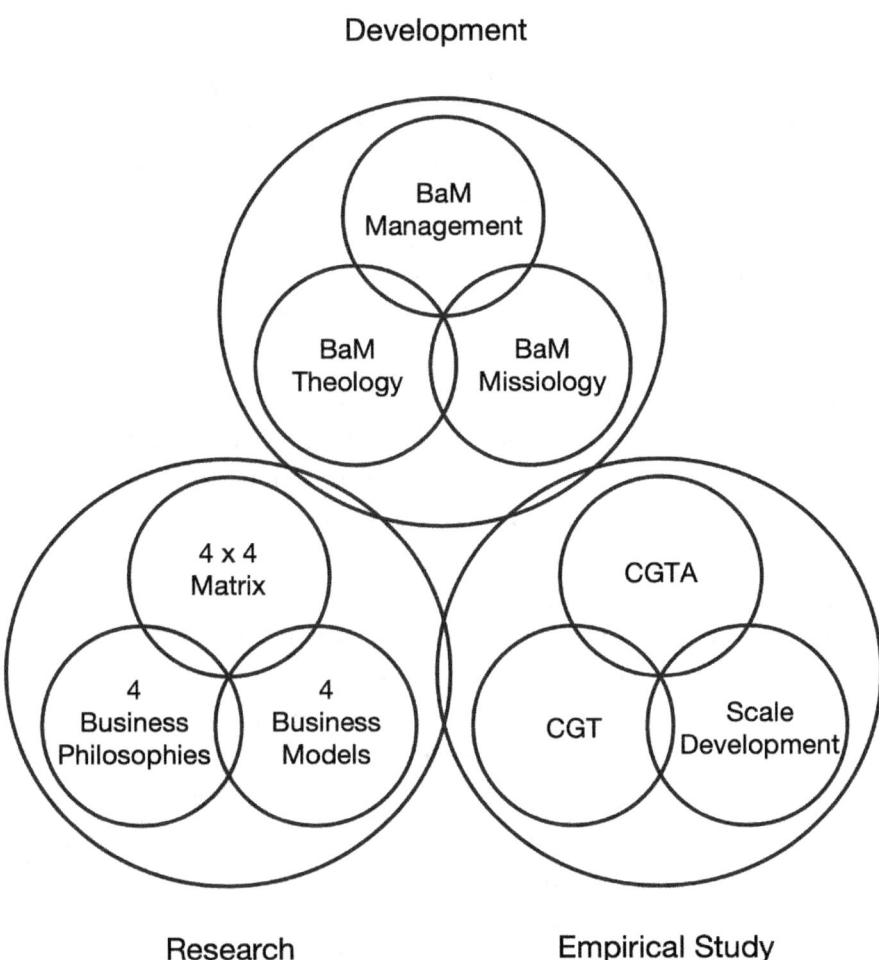

PREFACE

This book began with a simple yet fundamental question: Can a for-profit business genuinely demonstrate the love of God and neighborly love in its everyday operations, rather than in a piecemeal or even haphazard way through periodic philanthropy, social responsibilities, or occasional mission trips? This question guided my doctoral research on "business as ministry" in rural Midwest America and formed the empirical and theological groundwork for this volume.

Over two years of fieldwork, I listened to farmers, entrepreneurs, employees, pastors, and community leaders share their experiences with planning, hiring, pricing, investing, forgiving, and enduring together. While their stories were diverse, a common pattern emerged. When a company treated profit as necessary but not ultimate, resisted exploiting its neighbors, and kept worship at the center of its decision-making, four forms of capital flourished together. Spiritual capital shaped purpose, prayer, and ethics. Social capital deepened trust, goodwill, and collaboration. Intellectual capital organized creativity, insight, brand, and systems. Financial capital provided the margin and liquidity needed for steady operations and intergenerational stewardship. I call this integration the Common Good Treasure.

The broader literature in theology, Catholic social teaching, Protestant views on vocation, stakeholder theory, and corporate finance have been grappling with similar tensions. Some models provide effective tools for capital discipline but offer a limited understanding of moral purposes. In contrast, others present rich visions of the common good but lack practical guidance for managers. In response to the knowledge gap, the first half of this book presents a 4×4 Matrix that aligns four business models with four "laws" of the moral field. This matrix serves as a framework for understanding where a business operates within the landscape of markets and institutions and suggests potential steps toward more sustainable, trustworthy, and ethical practices.

The empirical study confirmed that a map alone is insufficient. Leaders also need instruments at their disposal to navigate effectively. Therefore, the second half of the book introduces two key concepts, the Common Good Treasure (CGT) and the Common Good Treasure Assessment (CGTA). CGT refers to the integrated spiritual, social, intellectual, and financial capital that God entrusts to an enterprise for the glory of God through the flourishing of individuals and communities. CGTA translates this concept into observable dimensions and presents it in a simple radar chart, allowing boards and teams to "test everything," engage in prayers, and take appropriate actions throughout the deliberate measurement process.

Volume 1 is intended for scholars and practitioners who are interested in precise constructs, transparent methods, and the responsible use of data. It traces the development from the Scripture's grand narrative to four business models, using a color-coded matrix and grounded qualitative findings, and culminates in an assessment framework. It connects disciplines that seldom interact, including biblical theology, missiology, qualitative research, business strategy, intellectual capital, and corporate finance. I hope this work serves as an interconnection for these fields, providing a common language that is both academically rigorous and easily understandable to guide practical applications.

In this four-book project, Volume 1 explains the "why." It defines the ocean, weather, geology, seas, treasures, and charts. Volume 2 translates this framework into practical, concise practices that individuals and teams can apply in real time. Volume 3 compiles exercises and case studies into a workbook for companies, classrooms, churches, and peer groups. Volume 4 provides a devotional prayerbook that anchors the entire journey in worship, confession, and shalom. Together, these volumes aim to create a community that measures in ways that respect individuals, publishes in ways that build trust, and acts in ways that strengthen both Kingdom orientation and value creation.

This book can be read either as a comprehensive argument or by focusing on specific chapters. Chapters 1 and 2 are particularly useful for those teaching Christian ethics, economics, or management. Chapter 3 offers a visual tool for research design and decision-making at the board level. Chapter 4 is of interest to qualitative researchers seeking to apply a constructivist and missional worldview in the field. Chapters 5 and 6 will benefit scholars focusing on measurement and practitioners who develop instruments for personal and organizational development. Finally, Chapter 7 outlines a research agenda and points toward the practical work in Volumes 2, 3, and 4.

As a fellow learner, I want to share my thoughts. My understanding of business, mission, and the common good has been continually shaped and corrected by the Scripture, mentors, and the enduring faith of those who steward resources such as land, shops, data, and money, often away from the spotlight. If this book holds any value, it is because it brings together their quiet wisdom and presents it in a lucid theological and managerial context.

My hope is that you will receive this volume as an invitation to a wondrous journey. May it help you see your work as a vessel in God's ocean, recognize your current position, and discern a faithful trajectory toward shalom. I pray that the Spirit uses these pages to align your scholarship, teaching, and practice with the love of God and the common good of your neighbors.

Eric Z.M. Ma
Newark, Delaware, U.S.A.

INTRODUCTION

Business as Ministry (BaM) integrates theology, missiology, and management, arguing that the daily operations of a business serve as a public witness to God's love and our love for neighbors. This volume presents the ideas clearly and succinctly for both scholars and practitioners. Drawing on biblical, theological, ethical, and managerial frameworks, we ensure that practical applications are informed and responsible. Our goal is straightforward—to define key terms, outline models, propose a diagnostic lens, and present a transparent method for measuring development and analyzing trends for different forms of capital.

We approach the Scriptures as a unified whole, reflecting on the themes of creation, fall, redemption, and new creation. We emphasize the common good as a central moral goal in economic life. In this framework, business is neither a necessary evil nor a purely secular activity. Rather, it is a vital component of society. Business serves as a platform for fulfilling one's vocation and demonstrating love for one's neighbors; however, it also requires discernment and a willingness to adapt. Therefore, we reject some common misconceptions. BaM is neither an addition to philanthropy nor a marketing strategy for corporate social responsibility. Additionally, it is not merely about meeting proselytizing quotas. Most importantly, BaM represents a way of organizing work, relationships, knowledge, and finance to promote the common good.

Chapter 1 situates BaM within the context of participating in God's mission and sets criteria for evaluating the moral legitimacy of any business model. Chapter 2 presents four operating models, i.e., Shareholder Wealth Maximization, Stakeholder Theory, the Common Good, and Business as Ministry, enabling readers to compare their normative and instrumental logics. Chapter 3 introduces the 4×4 Matrix, which integrates these models with four principles of the moral field, i.e., Jungle, Exchange, Moral

Sentiments, and Gratuitousness. This matrix makes the diagnostic process concrete, easy to understand, and reproducible.

Chapter 4 emphasizes that discernment without measurement can lead to a lack of focus and direction. We will explore measurement principles that support healthy development and avoid being punitive. Chapter 5 defines the Common Good Treasure (CGT), which comprises four types of capital, namely, Spiritual, Social, Intellectual, and Financial. Together, these elements form the foundation of an enterprise. Chapter 6 introduces the Common Good Treasure Assessment (CGTA), a formative tool aligned with the CGT. The assessment summarizes domain scores and helps us visualize them in a radar chart with a balanced interpretive band. Throughout the assessment process, we adhere to established testing standards regarding purpose, construction, caution, and consequences of use.

Chapter 7 integrates posture and governance. We embrace servantship, emphasizing a service-oriented approach that underpins effective stewardship. We also advocate fair processes and the principle of subsidiarity as essential guidelines for boards and executives. Furthermore, this chapter outlines a research and development agenda and sets the stage for Volume 2, a practical workbook that translates these concepts into standard operating procedures, regular practices, and performance dashboards.

We adhere to a clear guiding principle throughout this volume: Profit, cash, debt, and assets are merely fuels, and they are not the ultimate goal. Finance should support the enterprise's mission rather than dictate it. Social trust is built through fair processes and equitable exchanges. Intellectual capital becomes lasting when supported by learning systems. Spiritual capital guides the organization to serve our communities and foster love for our neighbors. When these four elements work in harmony, companies can genuinely act as credible advocates for the common good.

Volume 1 is intended for scholars who appreciate rigorous arguments, versatile methods, and responsible applications. Volumes 2, 3, and 4 will be geared toward practitioners. We hope that together, these four volumes will help communities develop balanced, truthful, and generous individuals and organizations in their daily work.

1
FOUR PHILOSOPHIES IN BUSINESS

1. FOUR PHILOSOPHIES IN BUSINESS

1.1 The Law of the Jungle

Anthropologists often use the "Law of the Jungle" to describe social worlds ordered by scarcity, power asymmetry, and fear. In such settings, groups prize dominance, security, and kin advantage. Cooperation is fragile and tends to collapse when trust is costly. Exchange tilts toward extraction, and status accrues to those who control resources or violence. Read through a business lens, this anthropology illuminates why some companies drift toward predatory behavior. They treat markets as zero-sum games, workers as expendable, and nature as a stock of inputs to be depleted. This pattern helps explain the hard edge of **shareholder-wealth-maximization (SWM)** when it is detached from countervailing norms, characterized by high-powered incentives, short horizons, and tolerance for negative externalities.

Yet even here, people still signal moral claims. They appeal to fairness, honor, and reciprocity, suggesting that "jungle" logics never completely erase human capacities for sympathy and gift. That tension prepares the reader for Chapter 2. Nonetheless, SWM names a real and powerful social logic. It is anthropologically intelligible, but it requires moral and institutional constraints if it is to serve the good of persons and communities (Van Duzer, 2010).

The biblical **grand narrative** portrays the Jungle as a distortion of a good creation (Gen. 1–2, NIV), intensified by the Fall (Gen. 3, NIV), resisted through God's mission in Israel's law and prophets, and decisively confronted by Jesus the Messiah, who forms a people to embody God's reign among the nations (Wright, 2025). Scripture affirms God's ownership of all creation (Ps. 24:1, NIV) and calls rulers to protect the vulnerable (Prov. 31:8-9, NIV). In Christ, domination gives way to servanthood (Mark 10:42-45, NIV), and the church's mission is to witness to the cruciform power that reconciles enemies and heals creation (Matt. 28:18-20, Col. 1:15-20, NIV).

When businesses mirror the Jungle's logics of exploitation, deceit, and ecological harm, the church names these as symptoms of the Fall and invites repentance toward practices that honor the Creator, neighbor, and land. This theological frame helps practitioners and scholars see why SWM, while analytically elegant, must be situated within a larger telos. Wealth is stewarded for worship, justice, and shalom, not worshiped as an end (Van Duzer, 2010; Wright, 2025).

In business managerial practice, the Jungle logic appears as pure **SWM**, unbounded by stakeholder claims. For example, it involves maximizing discounted cash flows, cutting costs aggressively, and privatizing gains amid socializing risks. While finance theory clarifies the tools (i.e., Net Present Value (NPV), Weighted Average Cost of Capital (WACC), and agency contracts), theology clarifies the aim (Benedict XVI, 2009; Van Duzer, 2010). Administrators can manage the Jungle dynamics by installing guardrails such as transparent governance, enforceable property rights and liability for externalities, and incentive designs that price long-horizon risk. Even within SWM, many managers adopt "no-go" zones (e.g., no deceptive marketing, no unsafe labor) because reputational, legal, and moral costs can swamp near-term gains.

Chapter 2 will analyze SWM as a coherent model and then show why ecologies of **Stakeholder Theory (ST)**, **Common Good (CG)**, and **Business as Ministry (BaM)** are needed to curb the Jungle tendencies and redirect enterprises toward human flourishing within God's mission (Freeman, 1984, 2010; Van Duzer, 2010; Wright, 2025).

1.2 The Law of Exchange

Across cultures, people exchange to reduce risk, broaden cooperation, and create value. Barter, credit, and money encode expectations of reciprocity and reputation. Markets are social technologies that aggregate dispersed knowledge and enable specialization. Properly governed, exchange channels self-interest toward mutual benefit. When poorly governed, it drifts toward opportunism.

This anthropology dovetails with **Stakeholder Theory (ST)**, which treats the enterprise as a nexus of relationships—employees, customers, suppliers, communities, and financiers. Cooperation among them creates surplus. Exchange, therefore, entails **mutual** claims, not merely contractual minimalism. Where SWM emphasizes residual claimants' returns, ST emphasizes relational capital such as trust, legitimacy, and shared purpose as productive assets. The law of exchange directs us to measure not only price and quantity, but also the quality of relationships and information flows that sustain cooperation over time (Donaldson & Preston, 1995; Freeman, 1984, 2010; Wong & Rae, 2011).

Biblically, exchange is embedded within the covenant. Land laws, honest weights, gleaning, Jubilee, and prohibitions against fraud signal God's desire for just markets that include the poor (Lev. 19; Deut. 24–25, NIV). In the grand narrative, Israel is called to model an alternative political economy for the nations. In Jesus, the kingdom reorders values around neighbor-love and truth-telling. In the church, mission unfolds through everyday work, trade, and generosity (Wright, 2025). The Apostle Paul's tentmaking shows how economic participation can advance witness without exploitation (Acts 18, NIV). Thus, ST resonates with Scripture's vision. Exchange is good when it honors persons as image-bearers, tells the truth, shares risks fairly, and preserves creation. Markets remain vital, yet missional faithfulness insists they be **morally formed**—not sacralized (Wong & Rae, 2011; Wright, 2006).

Administratively, the Law of Exchange translates into ST practices such as mapping stakeholders, clarifying material impacts, designing value propositions that co-create benefits, and establishing grievance and learning loops. Contract design should blend incentives with transparency and dispute resolution. Metrics should capture churn, supplier on-time-in-full, employee engagement, and community consent, not merely Earnings Per Share (EPS). Where SWM prizes short-term spread, ST prizes resilient cash flows rooted in trust.

In Chapter 2, we will show how ST's descriptive, instrumental, and normative strands (Donaldson & Preston, 1995) can align with finance (e.g., lower beta via stakeholder stability) while elevating the moral horizon of exchange (Freeman, 1984, 2010; Wong & Rae, 2011).

1.3 The Law of Moral Sentiments

Adam Smith argued that markets rely on moral emotions such as sympathy, resentment of injustice, and a desire for praise, well before they rely on prices (Smith, 1759). People internalize norms of fairness and dignity. They punish cheating and reward trustworthiness. These sentiments shape what counts as a "fair price," whether a layoff is perceived as just, and how communities grant or withdraw legitimacy.

In modern enterprises, they operate through culture, purpose, and leadership examples. This law points beyond exchange to the **formation** of persons and practices. It charts a path from ST to the **Common Good (CG)** model. Production should yield "good goods," "good work," and "good wealth," integrating moral sentiments into strategy rather than treating them as after-the-fact

Public Relations (PR) (McVea & Naughton, 2021; Wong & Rae, 2011). The anthropology here suggests that moral formation is not an optional add-on. On the contrary, it is a precondition for sustainable cooperation.

The grand narrative deepens Smith's intuition. As humans bear God's image, moral sentiments are creational gifts. Unfortunately, they become skewed after the Fall. With Christ, they can be renewed by grace. Through the work of the Spirit, communities can learn cruciform love (Gen. 1:26–28; Rom. 12:1–2; Gal. 5:22–23, NIV; Wright, 2006). The church's mission is to embody these renewed sentiments publicly, such as truthfulness in contracts, patience in negotiations, and generosity toward the vulnerable, so that the nations glimpse God's wisdom.

In business terms, **CG** treats profit as a means, not an end; work as a vocation; and wealth as a resource for justice and joy (Benedict XVI, 2009). Moral sentiments thus move beyond private piety to institutional design. Fair compensation, participatory decision-making, and stewardship of creation are acts of worship that serve God's mission (McCann, 2011; Wright, 2025).

Organizationally, the Law of Moral Sentiments functions as an operating system. It codifies purpose, aligns structures, and rewards behaviors that advance **CG** outcomes. "Good goods" meet real needs without deception. "Good work" develops people and respects subsidiarity. "Good wealth" balances wealth creation with just distribution and long-term stewardship (Benedict XVI, 2009; McVea & Naughton, 2021). Governance should integrate virtue metrics, such as safety, learning, inclusion, and ecological footprint, alongside financial metrics. Last but not the least, culture shapes the durability of performance.

In Chapter 2, the CG analysis will show how companies can treat moral sentiments as productive capital that lowers transaction costs, attracts talent, and earns durable community trust, yielding resilient value without capitulating to Jungle or Exchange reductionism (Smith, 1759; Wong & Rae, 2011; Wright, 2025).

1.4 The Law of Gratuitousness

Beyond exchange stands **the gift**. Every society knows practices in which value is given without immediate equivalence. For example, hospitality, mentoring, risk-sharing in crisis, patient capital for artisans, and environmental restoration for future generations. The gift does not abolish markets but underwrites them by seeding trust and solidarity.

In corporate life, gratuitousness appears in the forgiveness of honest error, open-source contributions, or investments with uncertain payback but clear communal benefit. These practices anticipate the **Business as Ministry (BaM)** model, which integrates profit and purpose through intentional generosity. Far from being "irrational," gifts often catalyze new exchanges and the thicker networks of reciprocity. Anthropology, therefore, suggests that gratuitousness is not the enemy of efficiency. Instead, it is the soil in which healthy markets grow.

The gospel announces that God gives before we can repay. Creation itself is a gift, redemption in Christ is sheer grace, and the Spirit empowers a people whose economic life is marked by **Caritas in Veritate**—love in truth (John 3:16; 2 Cor. 8–9, NIV; Benedict XVI, 2009). Wright's grand narrative discussion shows that God's mission forms a community whose generosity signals the Kingdom to the nations, bringing a blessing to all families of the earth and culminating in new creation (Gen. 12:1–3; Rev. 21–22, NIV; Wright, 2025).

McCann (2011) calls this the "principle of gratuitousness," inviting businesses to embed the logic of gift within production and exchange, not merely philanthropy. This theological vision animates **BaM**, which holds that businesses operate profitably and ministerially, offering goods, dignifying work, discipling owners and employees, and serving places as an act of worship and witness (Van Duzer, 2010; Wong & Rae, 2011; Ma, 2024).

In management terms, gratuitousness becomes a design choice. Enterprises develop pricing that protects the poor, human resources (HR) policies that prioritize development and Sabbath-like rest, supply chains that honor creation, and investment screens that favor communities most in need. BaM leaders adopt an optimal capital equilibrium and transparent governance to prevent drifting toward mere philanthropic branding. They measure social and spiritual outcomes alongside cash flows and treat profit as a fuel for missions, not the finish line.

Chapter 2 will model BaM's capital flows. It describes how worship reorients strategy, how discipleship shapes culture, and how generosity compounds stakeholder trust, while showing complementarities and tensions with SWM, ST, and CG. When done well, gratuitousness does not negate finance. Conversely, it redeems it for the sake of people and places in the light of God's mission (Benedict XVI, 2009; McCann, 2011; Van Duzer, 2010; Wright, 2006).

2
FOUR MODELS IN BUSINESS

2. FOUR MODELS IN BUSINESS

The operational dynamics of a business, from its core mission to diverse strategies, are fundamentally shaped by its internal framework, known as the business model. Massa et al. (2017) describe a profit-driven organization's business model as a blueprint that outlines its structure and mechanisms for achieving goals across economic, social, spiritual, ecological, and cultural domains (p. 1). A business model integrates three key components, i.e., purpose, structure, and process (Geissdoerfer et al., 2017). These elements are rooted in a divine foundation, reflecting how God's benevolence manifests through entrepreneurial talents.

Novak (1990) highlights that the true capital of an enterprise lies in its human creativity, knowledge, and ideas, which serve as catalysts for unlocking valuable assets in business endeavors. Insights from individuals are a company's most valuable resource, whereas wealth alone does not constitute capital. Indeed, the transformation of tangible assets depends on a deep understanding. Human knowledge represents true value and those who leverage it effectively emerge as capitalists. As Novak (1990) points out, the power of insight is transformative and impactful (p. 42), shaping businesses and empowering communities to thrive, as illustrated in Figure 3.

2.1 The Shareholder Wealth Maximization Model

The shareholder-wealth-maximization (SWM) paradigm is typically grounded in agency theory and property rights claims that delegate to managers a fiduciary duty to maximize residual returns to equity owners (Jensen & Meckling, 1976). Building on this framework, advocates contend that profit maximization is both descriptively accurate and normatively justified because it channels capital toward higher-valued uses and thereby promotes aggregate welfare

Figure 3. The Fundamental Capital Flow Map

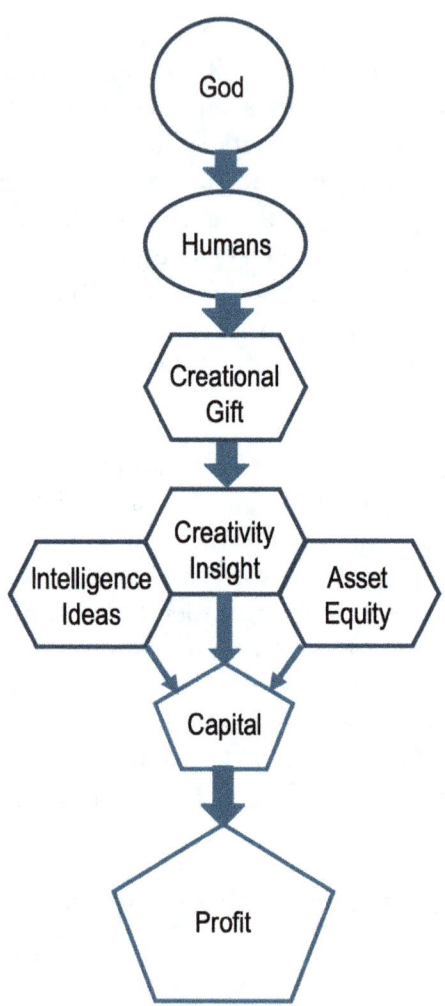

(Friedman, 2007; Sundaram & Inkpen, 2004; Windsor, 2010).

Yet the literature also registers deep tensions. Sison and Fontrodona (2011) argue that the classic "self-interest → common good" thesis is fragile. It privileges material metrics (e.g., assets, profits) while marginalizing relational goods (e.g., community, justice), risking the treatment of persons and places as means to shareholder ends. Van Duzer (2010) notes that within SWM, investments in employees or communities are warranted only when they raise profits—an instrumental logic that can crowd out genuinely moral reasoning.

Empirically, Yahanpath and Joseph (2011) link an uncompromising SWM orientation to behaviors evident in the 2007–2009 financial crisis (i.e., excessive leverage, and pay structures rewarding short-term risk-taking). Theologically, recent work emphasizes that wealth creation is a creational good, but it becomes disordered when "security" and status are absolutized. Leaders must distinguish legitimate human needs from the temptations of accumulation (McLeod, 2025). Read together, these points suggest that SWM delivers allocative clarity and market discipline, but without a thicker moral anthropology it easily slides into reductive decision rules and attenuated accountability to non-owner stakeholders (Friedman, 2007; Jensen & Meckling, 1976; Sison & Fontrodona, 2011; Sundaram & Inkpen, 2004; Van Duzer, 2010; Windsor, 2010; Yahanpath & Joseph, 2011).

The SWM Model Capital Flow Map in Figure 4 depicts a cascade that begins with God as the fountain of all gifts and descends to humans, whose image-bearing endowments—creativity/insight, intelligence/ideas, and asset/equity—seed the enterprise. Solid medium lines show these endowments consolidating into capital, which a thicker solid connector then carries into profit, signifying the model's controlling operational conduit. From profit, the dominant thick line runs to financials and to shareholders, visually encoding the model's telos. Managerial choice is finally evaluated by its impact on shareholder wealth.

Figure 4. SWM Capital Flow Map

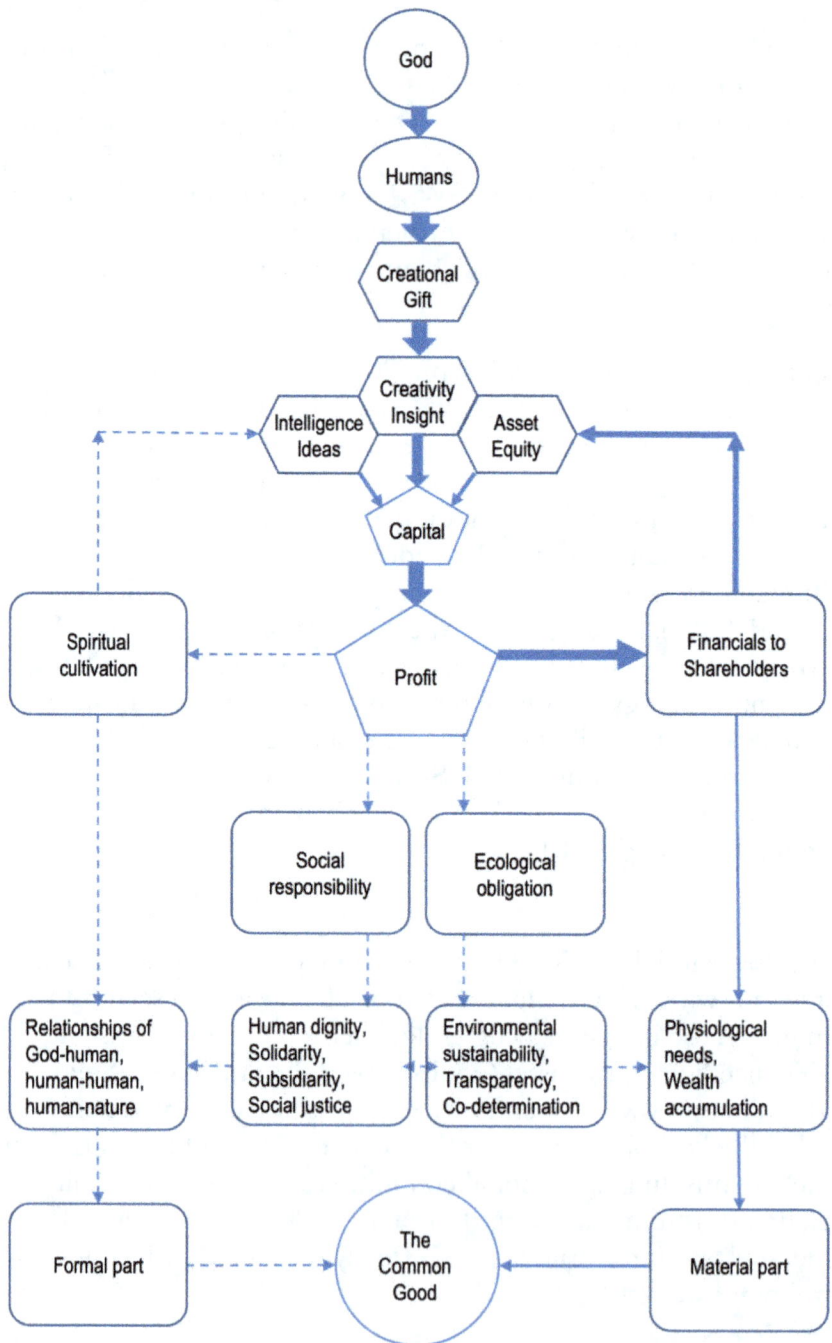

By contrast, thinner dotted lines trace secondary, conditional pathways—spiritual cultivation, social responsibility, and ecological obligation—that register moral considerations yet do not govern the flow. They serve as guardrails or constraints rather than coequal ends. The map also distinguishes the "formal part" (purpose, governance, intention) from the "material part" (assets, operations), suggesting that even when enterprises acknowledge obligations to community or creation, those concerns are typically filtered through profitability tests before capital is withheld, redeployed, or distributed (Van Duzer, 2010; Sundaram & Inkpen, 2004).

A theologically integrated interpretation thus affirms the good of productive surplus while warning against wealth hoarding and the eclipse of neighbor love. The SWM flow should be considered as a stewardship under God, or else the thick arrows toward shareholder gain can overpower the dotted lines of justice and care (Windsor, 2010; Sison & Fontrodona, 2011; Yahanpath & Joseph, 2011).

In sum, the map's thickness hierarchy and dotted feedback indicate SWM's grammar of capital → profit → shareholder returns as the commanding pathway, with other goods acknowledged but subordinated.

2.2 The Stakeholder Theory Model

The contemporary Stakeholder Theory (ST) tradition traces back to the Stanford Research Institute's 1963 use of "stakeholder," crystallized by Freeman's *Strategic Management: A Stakeholder Approach* (1984), which reoriented managerial purpose from a shareholder-only mandate to a vocation accountable to all parties with legitimate stakes in the business (Freeman, 1984; Freeman & Reed, 1983). The operative claim is not simply additive—"care for shareholders and everyone else"—but integrative. Value creation is relational, multidirectional, and institutionally embedded. Thus, contemporary articulations identify shareholders alongside employees, suppliers, local communities, creditors, society (social responsibility), and the

Figure 5. ST Capital Flow Map

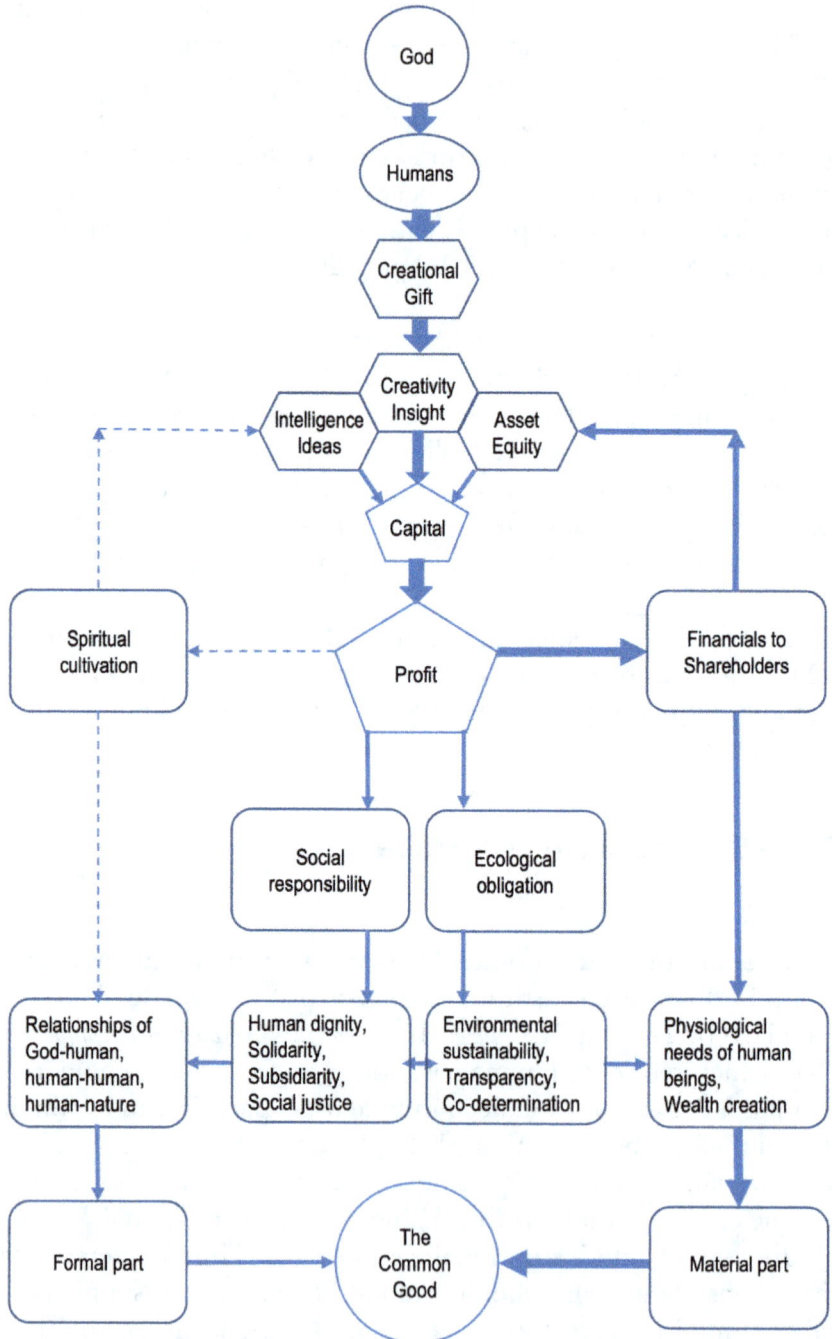

natural environment (ecological responsibility) as principals to whom managers owe due regard (Lin, 2018).

At the strategy level, ST coheres with both market-based and resource-based views. Companies must meet genuine customer needs while stewarding distinctive capabilities and assets through relational cooperation (Dawar, 2013; Grant, 1991; Phillips et al., 2019). Analytically, Donaldson and Preston (1995) distinguish descriptive (what companies do), instrumental (how stakeholder practices affect outcomes), and normative (what companies ought to do) dimensions, with the normative core grounding obligations in the moral standing of stakeholders rather than in their instrumental usefulness.

Theologically, this normative core resonates with a creational anthropology. Since persons and places are gifts of God, managerial authority is ministerial stewardship ordered to neighbor-love and the common good, not private aggrandizement. The ST Model Capital Flow Map in Figure 5 visually encodes this synthesis by situating economic reasoning within moral and relational terrains ["formal" (governance/intent) and "material" (assets/operations)], and by naming virtues such as transparency, co-determination, solidarity, and social justice as constitutive of corporate purpose. To that extent, ST does not reject profitability. It disciplines it within a horizon of human dignity, ecological care, and worshipful stewardship that treats profit as a servant, not sovereign (Donaldson & Preston, 1995; Freeman, 1984).

The ST Model Capital Flow Map in Figure 5 portrays capital's journey beginning in God, flowing as a creational gift to humans, whose image-bearing capacities—creativity/insight, intelligence/ideas, and asset/equity—seed the enterprise (solid, medium lines). From these endowments, the company aggregates capital, which thick solid arrows carry into profit, signaling the principal economic conduit by which investment becomes return. Unlike a shareholder-primacy schema that treats this conduit as the telos, ST embeds it within a wider network of dotted feedback lines—human dignity, solidarity, subsidiarity, social justice; relationships of God–human, human–human, human–nature; environmental sustainability, transparency, co-determination—that norm and redirect cash flows toward shared flourishing.

Practically, this means profits are governed and distributed through both "formal" (policies, purpose statements, decision rights) and "material" (assets, supply chains, labor practices) parts so that spiritual cultivation, social responsibility, ecological obligation, and financial returns to shareholders stand together as co-equal claims on enterprise surplus, not rival claimants. Managers, therefore, evaluate choices not only by expected returns but also by stakeholders' well-being and long-run value creation consistent with ST's descriptive, instrumental, and normative directives (Donaldson & Preston, 1995). Strategically, market-based attention to authentic customer needs and resource-based stewardship of distinctive capabilities shape where capital is allocated, while stakeholder relationships act as multipliers of intangible capital (e.g., trust, reputation, knowledge) that sustain competitive advantage (Phillips et al., 2019; Dawar, 2013; R. M. Grant, 1991).

Theologically, the map's architecture invites leaders to receive capital as a trust, configure operations as service to neighbors and places, and measure success by the common good rather than by shareholder gain alone. Profit is viewed as a means of love enacted across the enterprise's web of relationships.

2.3 The Common Good Model

The Common Good model draws on a long tradition in Catholic Social Teaching and aligns with Protestant work on vocation and stewardship. It reframes the end of a business as the common good and treats profit as a necessary means, not the final purpose (Faldetta, 2012; Felber et al., 2019; McVea & Naughton, 2021; Rieger, 2015; Rourke, 1996; Sison & Fontrodona, 2011, 2013). Building on Caritas in Veritate, McCann (2011) and Faldetta (2012) describe economic exchange as marked by gratitude and gift, reorienting contracts and prices toward mutual benefit. Sison and Fontrodona (2011) distinguish the "material part" of an enterprise's common good (its assets and profits) from the "formal part" (its relationships, purpose, and practical wisdom), clarifying that wealth creation belongs within, not above, a moral ecology of work. McVea and Naughton (2021) operationalize this vision with three integrating principles—**good goods** (meeting real needs and showing solidarity with the poor), **good work** (honoring the dignity of workers and practicing subsidiarity), and **good wealth** (creating wealth and distributing it justly). These proposals provide interpretive anchors for reading a capital flow map that aims at shared flourishing rather than a single claimant's gain.

For Protestant voices, Van Duzer (2010), Chalmers (2010), and Turnbull (2020) emphasize gratuitousness, reconciliation, and love for neighbors as the moral horizon of an enterprise. Related work highlights cooperative workplaces, dignified treatment, and care for creation as normal business practices (Wong & Rae, 2011; Wookey et al., 2023).

The CG Capital Flow Map in Figure 6 begins with God and the creational gift God gives. That gift flows to humans. Within the human block, the map lists the specific capacities and endowments that seed an enterprise—creativity/insight; intelligence/ideas; asset/equity. Solid connectors link these items to capital, showing how personal capacities and owned resources become investable means. From capital, a thicker solid arrow runs to profit, marking the main operating channel that any business must manage. From profit, the map widens. It shows four concrete uses of surplus—spiritual cultivation, social responsibility, ecological obligation, and financials to shareholders—with wealth creation explicitly named. These outputs span the map's "formal part" (purpose, governance, intent) and "material part" (assets, operations), signaling that both decisions and dollars matter.

The solid pathways and surrounding fields name the moral grammar that guides the flow—human dignity, solidarity, subsidiarity, social

Figure 6. CG Capital Flow Map

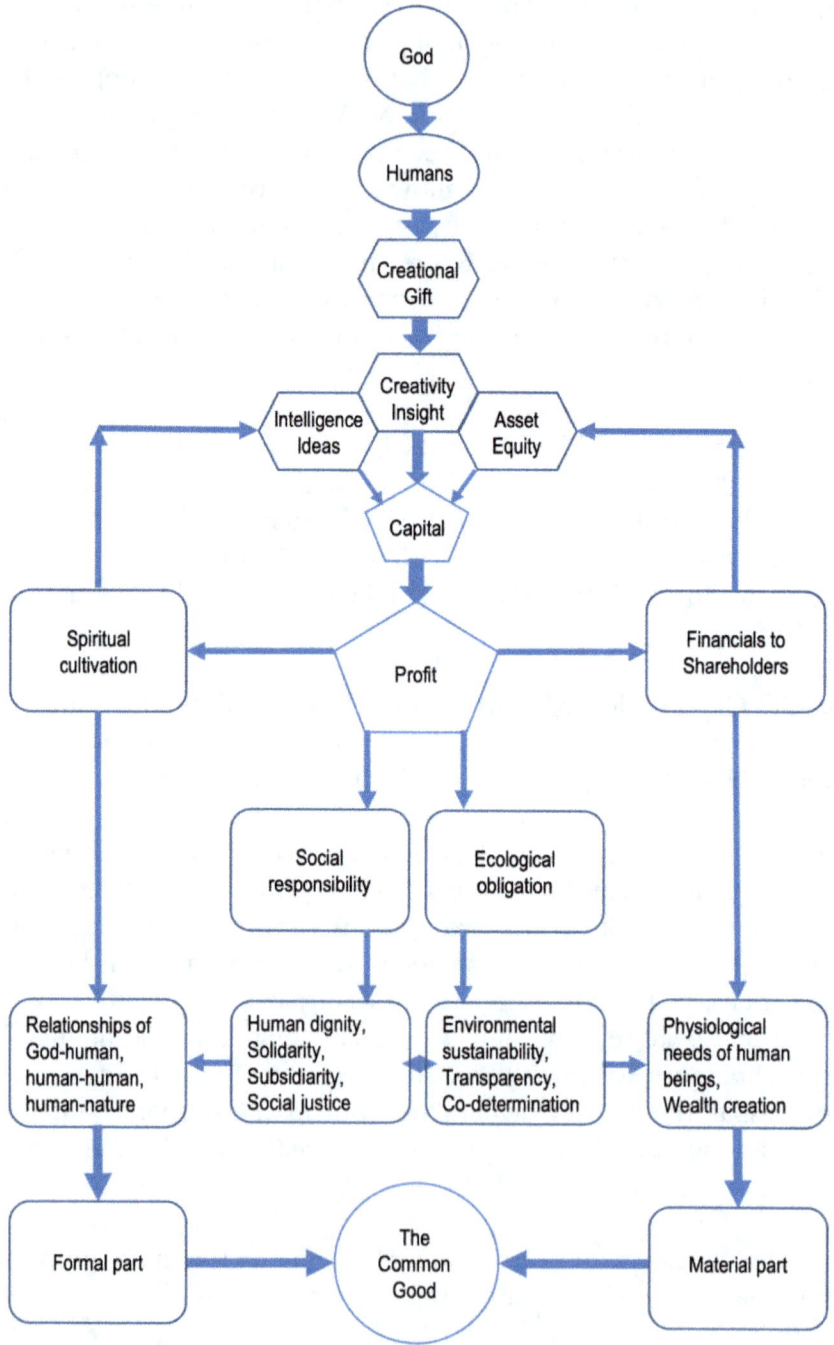

justice; environmental sustainability, transparency, co-determination; and the relationships of God–human, human–human, human–nature. The map also notes the physiological needs of human beings, a reminder that capital serves real people with real needs. All these streams converge in The Common Good as the telos of an enterprise.

The diagram emphasizes that cash moves along a necessary economic conduit (capital → profit), but feedback from persons, communities, and creation disciplines the direction and distribution of that cash so that good goods, good work, and good wealth are delivered together (McVea & Naughton, 2021; Sison & Fontrodona, 2011).

2.4 The Business as Ministry Model

The Business as Ministry (BaM) Model, as articulated in Ma's 2024 study, synthesizes corporate theology, common-good traditions, and contemporary strategy into an operating system for faith-driven enterprises (Ma, 2024). In Ma's account, an enterprise's resources are not only inputs for private gain but gifts to be received, refracted to neighbors, and reflected in worship, so that profit serves—rather than defines—the enterprise's end (Ma, 2024). This framework is grounded in Novak's "theology of the corporation," the common-good tradition of Sison and Fontrodona, and practical wisdom in Business as Mission scholarship. It draws on works from social and intellectual capital as well as corporate finance to discipline value creation (Brealey et al., 2020; Gort, 2018; Johnson, 2011; Marr, 2018; Novak, 1990; Sison & Fontrodona, 2011, 2013; Van Duzer, 2010; Wright, 2025).

Ma locates Business as Ministry (BaM)'s purpose in the "common good treasure" (CGT)—the optimal integration of spiritual, social, intellectual, and financial capital—and identifies "instruments of

Figure 7. BaM Capital Flow Map

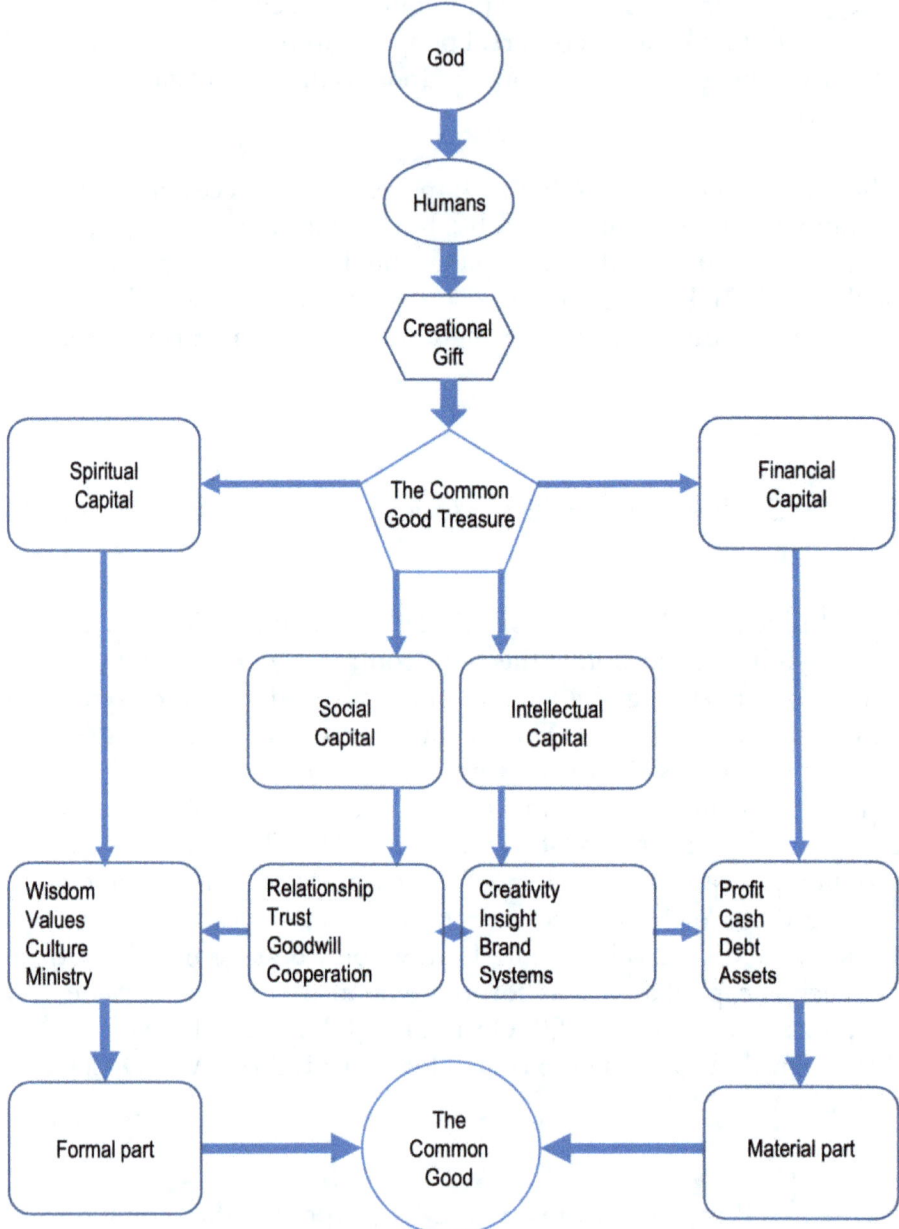

grace" (receiving, refracting, reflecting), three governing laws (exchange, moral sentiments, gratuitousness), and integrated strategies (market-, resource-, sociopolitical-, and CGT-based) as the model's conceptual core (Ma, 2024). These constructs are summarized in the capital flow map that anchors the model's interpretation for practitioners and scholars, translating theological purpose into managerial process.

Qualitative fieldwork in the U.S. rural Midwest further corroborates the model's categories and practices, showing how goodwill, trust, creativity, brand, systems, cash, debt, assets, and profit can be stewarded for shared flourishing (Ma, 2024). Notably, BaM advances the literature by moving from "why" to "what and how," integrating classical moral theology with contemporary strategy so that profit funds ministry and ministry governs profit (Ma, 2024).

The BaM Capital Flow Map in Figure 7 begins with God → Humans → Creational gift, positioning business within a received order rather than mere self-assertion (Ma, 2024). From this source, three human endowments flow toward enterprise building—intelligence/ideas, creativity/insight, and assets/equity. These inputs are gathered as capital, which is then used to generate profit—a necessary means but not the final goal. Profit, cash, debt, and assets do not end with shareholders. They are reinvested to develop the Common Good Treasure across four domains, each with a specific focus—Spiritual Capital (wisdom, values, culture, ministry), Social Capital (relationships, trust, goodwill, cooperation), Intellectual Capital (creativity, insight, brand, systems), and Financial Capital (profit, cash, debt, assets) (Ma, 2024).

In practice, wisdom and values influence governance and discernment; culture and ministry shape vocation and outreach; relationships and trust lower transaction costs; goodwill and cooperation foster resilient teams and partnerships; creativity and insight advance product and process innovation; brand and systems support learning at scale; profit and cash ensure liquidity, and debt and assets expand capacity (Ma, 2024).

These flows are guided by instruments of grace, i.e., receiving (to self), refracting (to others), and reflecting (on God), and managed through integrated strategies (market, resource, sociopolitical, and CGT-based) that align commercial decisions with community well-being. This creates a repeatable cycle of gifted endowments → capital formation → profit → CGT growth → renewed endowments, all directed to God's glory and love for neighbor. The map offers a visual framework for this cycle, helping leaders allocate resources to each element in every section with theological clarity and practical simplicity (Ma, 2024).

3
A 4×4 MATRIX IN BUSINESS

3. A 4×4 MATRIX IN BUSINESS

3.1 The 4×4 Matrix

A 4×4 Matrix overlays **four philosophies of doing business**—*the Law of the Jungle, the Law of Exchange, the Law of Moral Sentiments, and the Law of Gratuitousness*—onto **four operating models**—*Shareholder Wealth Maximization (SWM), Stakeholder Theory (ST), the Common Good (CG), and Business as Ministry (BaM)*. To help readers "see" the ocean of business, the matrix uses a **warm-to-cool color spectrum** to signal ethical and relational temperature in a business that aims to serve as a Christian ministry. **Warm reds and purples** flag extractive risk and high self-protection; **yellows and ambers** mark transactional equilibrium; **blues and aquas** suggest gift and grace; and **greens** indicate trust, reciprocity, virtue, and integrative shalom, as illustrated in Figure 8.

The palette moves from hot hues in the lower-left to cool greens in the upper-right, signaling a theological and managerial journey from anxious self-assertion toward reconciled, life-giving stewardship from creation's fracture to new-creation shalom in the arc of the biblical grand narrative (Wright, 2025). Reading from left to right within each row and from bottom to top within each column represents increasing participation in God's mission for the flourishing of persons, enterprises, and communities.

The matrix serves as a diagnostic tool, enabling readers to identify their organization's current "home cell" and chart a path toward more faithful practices. Organizations in the **Jungle** row operate with extractive practices combined with high self-protection, prioritize short-term gains, and insulate themselves from accountability and external scrutiny.

Figure 8. The 4×4 Matrix color semantics

Philosophy \ Model	Shareholder Wealth Maximization (SWM)	Stakeholder Theory (ST)	Common Good (CG)	Business as Ministry (BaM)
The Law of Gratuitousness (Gift)	Strategic Generosity	Distributed Benevolence	Gift-Ordered Firm	Shalom Enterprise
The Law of Moral Sentiments (Ethics)	Ethical Profit	Virtue Governance	Relational Common Good	Missional-Virtue Enterprise
The Law of Exchange (Trade)	Deal-Driven Returns	Reciprocal Stakeholding	Fair-Exchange Flourishing	Covenantal Commerce
The Law of the Jungle (Power)	Raw-Power Profit	Guarded Stakeholding	Constrained Common Good	Providence-Aware Enterprise

Jungle×SWM (red) businesses prioritize speed, control, and earnings per share. Leadership relies on agency theory tools and cost-of-capital thresholds (e.g., NPV/EPS/WACC), and social engagement is essentially a risk management (Jensen & Meckling, 1976; Friedman, 1970/2007).

Jungle×ST (vermilion) still concentrates power but manages coalitions to secure a "license to operate," with stakeholder dialogue serving as an insurance against backlash (Freeman, 1984/1983).

Jungle×CG (amber) accepts the limits on power. Legal and civic norms temper monopoly rents, yet the common good is primarily about compliance.

Jungle×BaM (yellow) often appears as a benevolent patriarch. Decisive owners deploy profits for philanthropy and evangelism, but governance remains centralized. The invitation is to loosen control and share agency for the mission.

In the **Exchange** row, companies operate on a transactional basis, seeking fair exchanges where value given roughly equals value received.

Exchange×SWM (purple) optimizes transactions across price, quality, and delivery as long as returns exceed the hurdle rate. Philanthropy is brand adjacent.

Exchange×ST (periwinkle) builds reciprocal partnerships and adopts triple-bottom-line reporting to align incentives (Freeman, 1984/1983).

Exchange×CG (mint) reframes exchange as a vehicle for "good goods, good work, and good wealth" (fair pricing, dignifying work, and just distribution) (McVea & Naughton, 2021).

Exchange×BaM (lime) becomes *covenantal commerce*. Contracts are honored but promises go further. Profit funds the growth of the spiritual, social, intellectual, and financial capitals of the "Common Good Treasure" (Ma, 2024).

In the **Moral Sentiments** row, companies weave empathy and virtue into daily practices.

Moral Sentiments×SWM (magenta) emphasizes character and compliance to curb opportunism while maintaining a shareholder mandate.

Moral Sentiments×ST (coral) strengthens procedural justice and trust.

Moral Sentiments×CG (pastel) normalizes subsidiarity and participation, enabling people to flourish (Sison & Fontrodona, 2011).

Moral Sentiments×BaM (chartreuse) aligns business practices with the missio Dei. Strategy is evaluated by its effects on the four "bottom lines" of spiritual, social, intellectual, and financial (Ma, 2024).

Finally, in the **Gratuitousness** row, organizations integrate trust, mutual exchange, ethical principles, and holistic harmony into their everyday practices.

Gratuitousness×SWM (deep blue) practices strategic generosity (cause marketing, and corporate giving) conditioned on ROI (Van Duzer, 2010).

Gratuitousness×ST (vivid blue) distributes benevolence through employee volunteerism and supplier development.

Gratuitousness×CG (aqua) embeds the gift logic of co-creation with the community and stewardship of the earth (Benedict XVI, 2009).

Gratuitousness×BaM (spring green) is the "Shalom

Enterprise." Profits are stewarded to grow the *Common Good Treasure* and reconcile relationships with God, neighbor, and creation (Wright, 2025; Ma, 2024; Sorenson & Milbrandt, 2023).

In sum, every contemporary business can be found in one of the sixteen cells. With theological imagination, an enterprise can intentionally move toward cooler, greener zones of durable prosperity and witness.

3.2 The Business Ocean

The quadrant overlay groups the 16 cells along two meta-gradients: **horizontal**—from *profit-primacy* (SWM→ST) to *mission-integration for the common good* (CG→BaM); **vertical**—from *power/trade* (Jungle→Exchange) to *ethics/gift* (Moral Sentiments→Gratuitousness), as shown in Figure 9.

Q1 (upper-left) gathers organizations with mission vocabulary but weak relational conversion, where paternalism or compliance risk persists (e.g., *Fair Exchange Flourishing, Covenantal Commerce*).

Q2 (upper-right) is the integrative horizon—organizations that embed *caritas* and reconciliation into strategy and governance (e.g., *Gift-Ordered Firm and Shalom Enterprise*).

Q3 (lower-left) focuses on the extractive or narrowly transactional plays (e.g., *Raw Power Profit, Guarded Stakeholding*).

Q4 (lower-right) features businesses that pursue virtue within profit guardrails (e.g., *Ethical Profit, Virtue Governance*).

Figure 9. The 4 Quadrants of the 4×4 Matrix color semantics

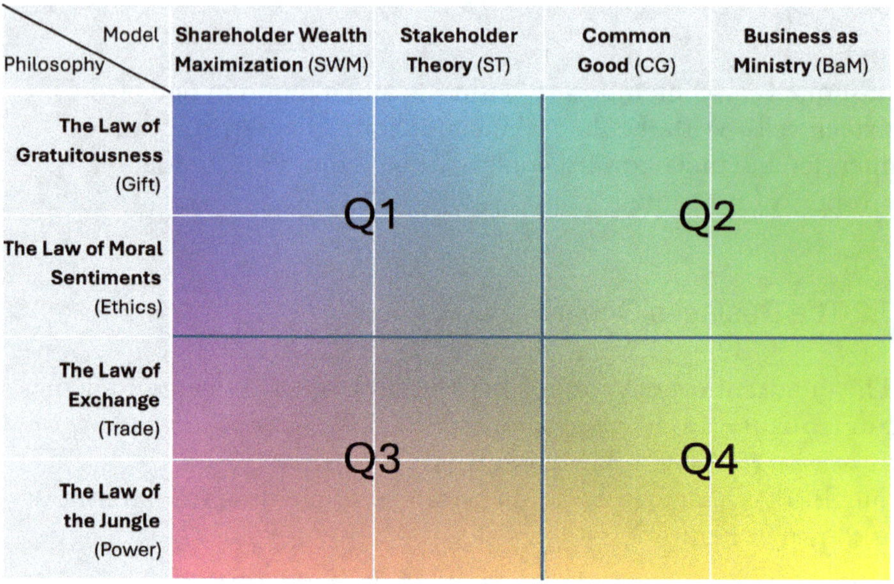

Philosophy \ Model	Shareholder Wealth Maximization (SWM)	Stakeholder Theory (ST)	Common Good (CG)	Business as Ministry (BaM)
The Law of Gratuitousness (Gift)	Q1		Q2	
The Law of Moral Sentiments (Ethics)				
The Law of Exchange (Trade)	Q3		Q4	
The Law of the Jungle (Power)				

Hot colors denote competitive intensity, thin relational capital, and short time horizons. Cooler blues and greens connote trust, just relationships, ecological attention, and long-run horizons that are key signals of a profitable business practiced as a Christian ministry (Van Duzer, 2010; Benedict XVI, 2009).

Theologically, the lower-left cells exemplify life "curved in on itself," whereas the upper-right cells witness to creation's healing in Christ, where profit becomes a means for "good goods, good work, and good wealth" ordered to the common good (McVea & Naughton, 2021).

Strategically, the columns recall the four models of Chapter 2, i.e., SWM's finance-first discipline (Jensen & Meckling, 1976; Friedman, 1970/2007), ST's multi-party accountability (Freeman, 1984/1983), CG's end-orientation to human flourishing (Sison & Fontrodona,

2011; Felber, 2019), and BaM's quadruple-capital stewardship oriented to God's mission (Ma, 2024). The matrix, therefore, offers both a diagnostic snapshot and a redemptive pathway for companies to move, cell by cell, toward shalom enterprises.

3.3 The Implication of the 4×4 Matrix

Three implications emerge from this framework. **First, the matrix integrates moral ends with managerial means**, dissolving the false dichotomy between "ethics" and "economics." By pairing models (columns) with guiding principles (rows), it shows that exchange without love leads to exploitation, while gratuitousness without discipline results in aimlessness. By incorporating the common good (CG column) and the missio Dei (BaM column) alongside shareholder and stakeholder perspectives, the framework encourages research on how capital budgeting, pricing, and governance evolve as companies shift "up and to the right" toward the more favorable cells (Sison & Fontrodona, 2011; Wright, 2006; Van Duzer, 2010).

Second, the matrix reframes the notion of performance. Scholarly work advocates multi-capital accounting, in which financial returns (ROIC over WACC) coexist with indicators of trust, participation, and ecological regeneration. The BaM approach introduces spiritual capital and mission integrity into the conversation (Rundle & Lee, 2022; McVea & Naughton, 2021; Felber, 2019). Empirical studies of family enterprises indicate that faith-based values enhance social capital, including trust, goodwill, and cooperation, which predict resilience in healthier business environments (Sorenson & Milbrandt, 2023).

Third, the matrix offers a missional theory of change. The color coding indicates directionality, helping managers envision "one-cell moves" through practices such as supplier development, participatory budgets, and sabbath rhythms that share agency and redistribute creative power for the benefit of neighbors and the community. This approach reflects the overarching narrative from creation to new creation (Gen 1–2; Rev 21–22) (Wright, 2025; Benedict XVI, 2009). For scholars, the grid clarifies ongoing debates. The normative claim of Shareholder Wealth Maximization (Friedman) and the instrumental/normative strands of Stakeholder Theory (Freeman) occupy distinct cells, enabling more precise hypotheses about outcomes as companies navigate toward shalom-oriented enterprises.

3.4 The Application of the 4×4 Matrix

A practical approach to using the matrix involves a three-step audit process.

Step 1—Identify Your Column (Model): Determine your operating discipline. If your focus is on maximizing shareholder returns (EPS/NPV relative to WACC), you likely fall under Shareholder Wealth Maximization (SWM). If you prioritize accountability to employees, suppliers, communities, and the environment through formal stakeholder engagement, you align with Stakeholder Theory (ST). If you view profit as a means to promote human flourishing under the principles of "good goods, good work, good wealth," you are part of the Common Good (CG) model. If your enterprise actively manages spiritual, social, intellectual, and financial capital as part of its mission, you belong to the Business as Ministry (BaM) category (Jensen & Meckling, 1976; Freeman, 1984/1983; McVea & Naughton, 2021; Ma, 2024).

Step 2—Discern Your Row (Philosophy): Consider your guiding principle. Do your decision-making processes resemble contests for power (Jungle), arm's-length transactions (Exchange), empathy-driven prudence (Moral Sentiments) (Smith, 1759), or practices rooted in generosity and charity (Gratuitousness), guided by truth (Benedict XVI, 2009)?

Step 3—Design a One-Cell Move: For example, a public company at Exchange×SWM might transition to Exchange×ST by implementing supplier prepayment for micro-vendors and publishing integrated stakeholder metrics. A company in the CG model at Moral Sentiments×CG may shift to Gratuitousness×CG by adopting a common-good balance sheet and introducing profit-sharing for low-wage workers (Felber, 2019). A family business at Exchange×BaM can progress to Moral Sentiments×BaM by establishing a rule of life centered on principles such as sabbath, forgiveness, and open-book management, fostering trust and goodwill that are key drivers of family social capital and long-term performance (Sorenson & Milbrandt, 2023).

This matrix can also guide board discussions (through quarterly check-ins on each cell), enhance capital budgeting (requiring proposals to detail impacts on all four capitals of the Common Good Treasure), and support talent development (emphasizing virtue formation alongside technical training). When used this way, the colors within the matrix serve as a pastoral guide for corporate sanctification. While profit remains a necessary resource, the guiding force is a deep love for God and neighbors, aimed at creating a glimpse of the new creation in the marketplace (Wright, 2025; Wong & Rae, 2011; Van Duzer, 2010).

4
FROM DISCERNMENT TO MEASUREMENT

4. FROM DISCERNMENT TO MEASUREMENT

4.1 Research Design

This chapter describes how the project transitioned from the moral vision outlined in Chapters 1–3 to an empirically grounded measurement approach. The dissertation posed a single and practical question: *How do stakeholders in profit-making firms practice and perceive "business as ministry" for the common good?* (Ma, 2024). Five sub-questions examined the financial, spiritual, social, and intellectual dimensions of everyday work, anticipating the four-capital framework developed later in this volume (Ma, 2024). Guided by a theological perspective that interprets business within the Bible's grand narrative—creation, fall, redemption, and new creation—the study assumed that commerce could engage in God's mission when properly oriented toward neighbor-love and the common good (Wright, 2006).

The research focused on the U.S. rural Midwest because its long-term stewardship, strong social networks, and clear faith commitments provide a living laboratory for integrating moral ends with management means. The design was a qualitative research study rooted in a social-constructivist worldview. The understanding of "business as ministry" is co-created by owners, employees, customers, suppliers, community leaders, and the researcher over time (Charmaz, 2014; Costantino, 2008; Creswell & Creswell, 2018; Glesne, 2016; Merriam & Tisdell, 2016).

The sample included 33 participants affiliated with 14 for-profit businesses—nine farms and five small businesses—selected through purposeful sampling to maximize variation across industry, role, and faith tradition (Ma, 2024). Over two years of immersion in the region along with extended site visits and repeated conversations, all this provided thick description and the trust necessary to observe "what a good business does" in financial and non-financial ways (Ma, 2024). Data sources including interviews, field notes, reflective memos, and archival materials were triangulated to verify interpretations and enhance credibility (Flick, 2022).

Collectively, the design operationalized the 4×4 vision from Chapter 3. It treated economic performance, stakeholder relationships, cultural meaning, and practical know-how as interconnected components while maintaining a clear focus on God's mission (Wright, 2006).

4.2 Why Constructivist Worldview, Qualitative Method, and Inductive Approach

A social constructivist worldview aligns well with both the topic and the theological commitments of this book. In Scripture's grand narrative, God forms a people and sends them as witnesses within cultures. Meaning emerges dialogically as humans respond to God and to one another in concrete settings (Wright, 2006). The study aimed to observe how farmers, shop owners, employees, and customers together understand business as a ministry and how that understanding influences practice. Constructivism, therefore, provided epistemic humility, reflexivity, and attention to situated meanings, all essential in a field where terms like "profit" and "ministry" are often debated (Creswell & Poth, 2018; Ma, 2024). A qualitative approach was chosen because the goal was understanding rather than causal analysis. The unit of analysis was the lived experiences of stakeholders across four interconnected domains rather than isolated variables (Ma, 2024; Merriam & Tisdell, 2016). The study adopted an inductive stance so that codes, categories, and themes emerged from the data through repeated reading, memoing, and participant engagement, rather than being based on preconceived constructs (Charmaz, 2014; Ma, 2024).

Trustworthiness was established through extended engagement, source triangulation, reflexive journaling, peer review, and member validation. Transferability was ensured by rich descriptions, dependability by maintaining an audit trail, and confirmability by systematically documenting analytic decisions (Creswell & Poth, 2018; Flick, 2022; Guba & Lincoln, 2000; Ma, 2024; Merriam &

Tisdell, 2016; Schwandt, 2015; Shenton, 2004). Ethical integrity was maintained through Institutional Review Board (IRB) approval, informed consent, confidentiality protocols, and careful handling of potentially identifiable information (Ma, 2024; Miles et al., 2018).

Methodologically, the study honors the 4×4 Matrix's first implication, "integrating moral ends with managerial means," by allowing stakeholders to narrate their performance, while theologically recognizing God's mission as the overarching framework that provides coherence to these narratives (Wright, 2006).

4.3 Field Procedures, Data, and Analysis

Fieldwork followed cycles of observation, interviewing, coding, and validation. Fourteen research sites were visited—comprising grain, vegetable, flower, and horse farms; a salon; real estate and logistics firms; an apparel micro-enterprise; and a health-tech startup—offering a range of organizational forms within one regional economy (Ma, 2024). Thirty-three interviews included owners, employees, customers, pastors, and a researcher connected to agriculture. Participants ranged in ages from 18 to 65+, representing multiple occupations and embracing fifteen faith traditions, ensuring diverse perspectives (Ma, 2024).

Observations produced detailed field notes on work practices, technology use (e.g., precision agriculture), and community interactions, often spanning full operating days (Ma, 2024). Audio recordings were transcribed using digital tools and verified manually. Artifacts such as budgets, historical newspapers, family histories, and newsletters enriched context and supported triangulation (Ma, 2024).

Analysis used Dedoose to manage a large dataset, encompassing 680 excerpts, 1,535 code applications, and 250 initial and focused codes, organized into 16 categories and ultimately four overarching themes (Charmaz, 2014; Creswell & Poth, 2018; Ma, 2024; Merriam & Tisdell, 2016; Saldaña, 2021). The "analysis spiral" progressed through memoing, constant comparison, and visual displays. Interim findings were shared with informants for member checks when appropriate (Ma, 2024). Credibility was enhanced through prolonged engagement, consistent observation, triangulation across 14 sites, peer debriefing, and attention to discrepant data. Transferability was supported by thick descriptions of settings and cases. Dependability and confirmability were maintained through an audit trail and the researcher's reflexive stance (Guba & Lincoln, 2000; Ma, 2024; Schwandt, 2015). Theologically, this approach allowed the "voices of the field" to identify both brokenness and grace in business, aligning with a missional hermeneutic that seeks signs of redemption within everyday economic labor (Wright, 2006). Overall, these procedures aimed to respect individuals, retain contextual integrity, and reveal patterns robust enough to guide subsequent measurement efforts.

4.4 Main Results and Implications

Four themes emerged that align with concerns recognized by scholars and practitioners, i.e., financial, spiritual, social, and intellectual capital (Ma, 2024). Financial capital centered on profit, cash, debt, and assets. Participants viewed profit as necessary but not the ultimate goal, characterized by having enough margin to support missions and intergenerational stewardship while constrained by conscience and community. Expressions such as "profit is a thing but not everything" reflected this ethic (Ma, 2024). Spiritual capital included the fear of the Lord, practical wisdom, values, culture, and hands-on ministries rooted in workplaces. Social capital emphasized relationships, trust, goodwill, and collaborative action that transform a business into a network of mutual care rather than a zero-sum game. Intellectual capital involves creativity, insight, branding, and systems that turn know-how into sustainable value (Ma, 2024).

Collectively, these insights highlight three key implications of the 4×4 Matrix. The first is "Integration," i.e., moral goals and management methods are interconnected. Study participants opposed formulas that prioritize any single capital, such as profit, at the expense of others. The second is "Performance." "Doing well" means not only maintaining liquidity and solvency but also building trust, showcasing wisdom in action, and codifying know-how. The third is "Missional change." Progress occurs when spiritual direction, social bonds, management systems, and financial resources realign to serve neighbors through love.

Practically, this suggests a need for an instrument that can: (1) identify an enterprise's current position within an integrated framework, (2) measure performance across all four capitals, and (3) monitor change over time without penalizing honest self-assessment. Therefore, Chapters 5 and 6 introduce an integrated model and a formative assessment to convert these qualitative insights into a practical and repeatable process for leaders and boards—always keeping God's mission as the guiding horizon for interpretation and action (Wright, 2025).

5
THE COMMON GOOD TREASURE

5. THE COMMON GOOD TREASURE

5.1 The Common Good Treasure

Christian tradition locates the *common good* in a moral and institutional order that enables persons and communities to flourish before God. Michael Novak's defense of democratic capitalism holds that markets serve the common good only when embedded in a broader moral ecology of culture and virtue, whereas Yves R. Simon's Thomistic lens emphasizes the bonum commune as shared ends and the civic conditions that make excellence possible (Rourke, 1996). In today's knowledge economy, the common good also depends on the responsible production and circulation of truth through "critical communities," linking intellectual life to public benefit (Longino, 2002). A Christian vision of business integrates these strands. Enterprises are called to create goods and services, provide meaningful work, and generate profit as stewardship toward shalom, developing right relationships with God, neighbor, and creation (Wong & Rae, 2011). In this book, we name the integrated fruit of such stewardship "The Common Good Treasure" (CGT). It is the ordered synergy of spiritual capital (the rudder), social capital (the adhesive), intellectual capital (the engine), and financial capital (the fuel), oriented to God's glory (Ma, 2024). (Remark: all names in the following case examples are pseudonyms.)

In Ma's study, Robert and Sarah run a horse farm that exemplifies CGT in practice. Socially, they cultivate *trust* through transparent operations, rigorous safety systems, generous training, and gratitude. At one point by gifting a long-serving hand a horse, they deepen employee loyalty and customer confidence (Ma, 2024). Intellectually, their know-how, teaching, safety protocols, and feedback loops function as a continuousimprovement engine. Financially, they manage cash by optimizing multi-year flows, including timed buying and selling of horses, to stabilize the venture while refusing exploitative practices (Ma, 2024). Spiritually, they pray with clients and staff, share a brief Scripture verse after each training lesson, host small Bible-study circles for students and parents, and cultivate an atmosphere that is genuinely safe and welcoming to people from diverse backgrounds. For years, "more and more men and women believed in the Lord and were added to their number" (Acts 5:14, NIV).

Care for creation is not a slogan but a practice in Robert and Sarah's horse farm—responsible stewardship of animals and the land. The results go beyond customer satisfaction. Trust deepens, community forms, and people encounter the beauty of God's handiwork in everyday work. The whole approach is animated by a moral commitment to honor people and animals before profit claims, which, over time, has yielded reputational goodwill in the community. In their hands, boarding becomes belonging, instruction becomes discipleship, and profit becomes provision for neighbors—a practical picture of a vessel carrying CGT in the rural Midwest, USA (Ma, 2024).

When the four capitals are properly ordered, a company does more than generate profit. It becomes a steward of what Scripture calls "true riches" (Luke 16:11, NIV). It sails with purpose, carrying CGT, bringing a blessing that overflows from the marketplace into families, communities, and nations. But when any of these capitals is missing or misaligned, the vessel falters. We see businesses brimming with innovation and financial strength yet morally adrift. Others are full of zeal but lack wisdom, wasting energy until entropy sets in. What keeps the vessel balanced? It begins with spiritual capital—the rudder that guides every other resource.

5.2 Spiritual Capital — Rudder

Spiritual capital is the inner "power, influence, and disposition" formed through a community's lived relationship with God. It includes beliefs, practices, and wisdom that guide all other resources (D'Souza, 2017). In the biblical imagination, gardens and gardeners figure prominently in God's redemptive work, reminding us that cultivation under God's hand shapes character, purpose, and fruit (John 15:18-20). This is a lens D'Souza extends by showing how gardening practices awaken discernment and reverent attention to the Creator's presence.

In organizational life, spiritual capital appears as values-guided decision-making, prayerful dependence, and service that release creativity and solidarity. However, it is easily suppressed by bottom-line-only cultures (O'Brien, 2017). Zohar and Marshall (2011) call this reservoir the "wealth we can live by," a deep meaning-system that orients risk, reward, and strategy toward the good. When spiritual capital is treated as the rudder in the "vessel," missional purpose (why we exist) governs managerial practice (how we budget, hire, and design products), aligning witness and performance (D'Souza, 2017; O'Brien, 2017).

Consider Elizabeth Tailor, a niche fashion business in the U.S. Midwest, founded by Elizabeth, a young fashion designer shaped by her family's faith and farming heritage. Amid the noise of the "fast fashion" industry, Elizabeth knelt in prayer, asking God how her business could reflect His values. What followed was not a trend forecast but a Spirit-led pivot of a "slow fashion." With intentional design, ethical sourcing, and sustainable tailoring, Elizabeth's shop became more than a boutique. It became a prophetic witness against consumerism. She offered repair services, educated her community on the environmental impact of slow versus fast culture, and fostered intergenerational conversations about stewardship. "God showed me that sustainability isn't a buzzword," she said, "it's discipleship—with a needle and thread." What Elizabeth lacked in venture capital, she made up for with spiritual clarity. Her brand thrived not through viral campaigns but through trust, craftsmanship, and care for creation. Like a rudder beneath the waves, her quiet yet deliberate spiritual convictions guided her business through stormy cultural currents (Ma, 2024).

After four decades in education, David and Barbara, Quakers shaped by a family lineage of enterprise, set aside part of their 11-acre homestead to grow roses, lilies, sunflowers, and dahlias for nearby farmers' markets. Their ethic of "profitable but not exploitative" flows from Quaker honesty and a long-term care for neighbors and land rather than short-term gain (Ma, 2024). In a season of relational strain, David built a simple wooden gate at the garden's entrance. Walking through it became a liturgy of "passing into a place of peace." When tensions arose, he and Barbara invited those involved to weed or harvest together in the sun. Conversation returned, forgiveness surfaced, and trust was rebuilt as hands worked the soil (Ma, 2024). Their practice mirrors D'Souza's account of gardening as a generator of *spiritual capital*. It is a stabilizing and energizing habit that awakens attentiveness to God and cultivates a "rooted, natural, and organic spirituality," translating inner renewal into ethical action (D'Souza, 2017). On this flower farm, the gate is more than décor. It marks the threshold where prayer meets pricing, where reconciliation guides market choices, and where cultivating beauty steers the firm's mission.

In both enterprises, spiritual capital served as a rudder. It set direction (purpose with God), corrected drift (repentance and reconciliation), and converted convictions into a distinctive strategy (brand, hiring, pace, and practices). Theology supplied the telos; missiology insisted that the witness be embodied; and management translated convictions into policies and rhythms.

"In all your ways acknowledge Him, and He will make straight your paths" (Proverbs 3:6). Without the rudder, a ship drifts. With it, even the fiercest headwinds can be navigated.

Next, we will turn from the rudder to the hull's cohesion, Social Capital: The Adhesive, to see how relationships, trust, goodwill, and cooperation hold the vessel together for the voyage.

5.3 Social Capital — Adhesive

If spiritual capital is the rudder, social capital is the adhesive that holds the vessel together. It binds teams in trust, weaves customers into loyalty, and anchors businesses in the goodwill of their communities. Without it, even the most brilliant strategy eventually fractures under relational strain. In Scripture, covenantal love and truthful speech form the social bonds that enable life together (Eph. 4:25; Col. 3:12–14, NIV). Catholic social teaching describes this "more-than-contractual" fabric as the logic of gift, a gratuitousness that complements market exchange and makes genuine cooperation possible in economic life (McCann, 2011). In practice, this grace-infused reciprocity appears as trust, dependability, and norm-keeping—the hallmark elements of social capital that lower transaction costs, accelerate adoption of change, and sustain collaboration (Lovrich & Pierce, 2016). Missiologically, trust is a witness. When a business embodies neighbor-love in policies and relationships, the watching community "tastes" the Kingdom.

Organizationally, faith-shaped family and company values become institutional assets. Repeated practices (such as forgiveness, shared prayer, fair dealing) compound into resilient networks that carry the enterprise through conflict and succession (Sorenson & Milbrandt, 2023). Their qualitative work with Christian-owned family businesses shows how faith practices reinforce ethical norms, which in turn generate durable social capital and measurable business outcomes including succession readiness, employee loyalty, and community support.

Sorenson and Milbrandt (2023) studied four Christian-owned family businesses and found a recurring pattern: Shared faith practices →

Internalized values → High family social capital → Stronger business performance. In one family, weekly prayer and Scripture at the dinner table evolved into a rule of life that governed the shop floor. The owners hosted quarterly "values forums" where cousins and non-family supervisors reviewed decisions against house norms of honesty, mutual respect, and generosity. Hiring and promotion emphasized value fit as much as technical skill. Over time, this reduced supervision costs and improved knowledge sharing. When a tense succession conversation surfaced, the family used its practiced habits of listening, confession, and reconciliation to reach consensus without litigation. Interviews and archives across the four families showed similar dynamics. Faith practices sustained values; values produced trust, goodwill, and cooperation; and social capital supported succession, performance, and community reputation (Sorenson & Milbrandt, 2023). Their theory of Faith-Based Family Business summarizes the following chain: Family faith → Family values → Family social capital → Enterprise outcomes. It is an arc that illustrates how "the adhesive" is made, not merely presumed.

In a low-trust context marked by corruption and exploitation, Protestant entrepreneurs in China reported that conversion reshaped how they build and extend trust at work (Tong & Yang, 2016). One construction owner employing 5,000 to 6,000 migrant workers faced hostility, vandalized dorms, and strained relationships. Because of his faith, he chose a different path. He founded on-site schools covering safety, legal literacy, and positive life skills. He upgraded cafeterias and housing and created a poverty relief fund for workers' families. Over time, employees articulated the trust dividend. They preferred slightly lower wages in exchange for the dignity, fairness, and "ease of heart" they experienced at his company (Tong & Yang, 2016). Across 43 interviews, Tong and Yang found that many Christian owners became more willing to be trustworthy, extended greater trust, and used religious ethics of integrity, fairness, and compassion to guide decisions that earned trust from employees and clients (Tong & Yang, 2016). The result was not soft management, but efficient cooperation, lower monitoring costs, and reputational strength grounded in moral consistency.

Theologically, gratuitous love supplies what contracts cannot. Missionally, trust embodies the good news in relational form. Managerially, social capital is an asset that compounds through repeated and value-consistent actions (McCann, 2011; Lovrich & Pierce, 2016). In the U.S. family enterprise, liturgies of prayer and confession matured into governance routines that stabilized succession (Sorenson & Milbrandt, 2023). In China, faith-motivated investments in worker dignity translated into organizational trust and efficiency (Tong & Yang, 2016). These stories confirm that the "adhesive" is cultivated through practices that align hearts and systems.

With the hull now held together, the vessel needs propulsion. Next, we will turn to Intellectual Capital: The Engine to see how God's wisdom, creativity, and systems thinking convert trusted relationships into insight, brand, and scalable execution for the common good.

5.4 Intellectual Capital — Engine

A vessel with a rudder and sound construction still needs an engine. Intellectual capital such as creativity, insight, brand, and systems, propels a business forward. But when intellectual capital is disconnected from spiritual capital, the engine may run fast yet in the wrong direction.

Below is an integration of theology, missiology, and business administration. In Scripture, wisdom is God's gift for faithful work, ordering love toward neighbor and creation (Prov. 2; Col. 1:9-10, NIV). In the marketplace, that wisdom becomes the *intellectual capital* —the human, structural, and relational know-how through which a company learns, designs, and serves (Marr, 2018). Theologically, this learning reflects the imago Dei. Missiologically, it advances human flourishing and witness as knowledge is shared for the common good. Strategically, leaders are stewards of these intangibles. They align vision, culture, and systems so that potential knowledge becomes replicable value for stakeholders (Shafique, Rafi, & Kalyar, 2021).

Bratianu (2025) clarifies why this stewardship is both spiritual and managerial. Rational, emotional, and spiritual knowledge generate corresponding forms of intellectual capital. Wise organizations translate potential intellectual capital into kinetic intellectual capital through disciplined knowledge management. In BaM terms, this engine comprising creativity, insight, brand, and systems runs best when spiritual knowledge (purpose, faith, and discernment) informs design, relationships, and execution, turning ideas into service for the common good.

In Ma's study, Joseph and partners owned proprietary computational medical-informatics intellectual property. Recognizing they were "intellectual-capital affluent," they built strategies that prioritized capitals. First intellectual, then financial, spiritual, and social, allocating resources to creativity, insight, brand, and systems before cash and debt, and then to values, culture, ministry, relationships, trust, and cooperation (Ma, 2024). Their choice reflects Bratianu's movement from potential to kinetic intellectual capital by stewarding protected knowledge (human/structural) through systems that deliver value and reinvesting results to grow spiritual and financial capital for mission. Missiologically, the product serves clinicians and patients. Organizationally, the brand signals trustworthy and purpose-driven technology. Spiritually, the firm's wisdom-seeking posture frames profit as the fuel for care.

Leased to a multigenerational farmer, the William Conservation Farm, a 130-year family holding, embodies intellectual capital as codified practice and partnership. The team institutionalized cover cropping (rye, oats, and radishes), no-till methods, saturated buffers, and woodchip bioreactors to reduce erosion and filter nutrients, while collaborating with external organizations to spread these practices (Ma, 2024). Here, human know-how becomes structural routines (i.e., systems), amplified by relational networks. The farm's conservation identity embodies a brand of "stewarding soil and water," turning tacit craft into explicit and transmissible knowledge that blesses neighbors downstream, modeling an example of kinetic IC deployed for local shalom.

Theologically, both enterprises show that spiritual intellectual capital of wisdom-infused knowing guides the engine. Joseph channels protected insight toward healing, while William codifies agronomic wisdom into systems that serve creation and community (Bratianu, 2025; Ma, 2024). Administratively, leaders convert potential into performance by aligning knowledge flows, culture, and structure (Marr, 2018; Shafique et al., 2021). Missiologically, the engine propels witness as value is created for patients, producers, and places.

Yet engines require fuel. The next section, Financial Capital: The Fuel, examines how profit, cash, debt, and assets sustain this wisdom-driven engine without distorting its purpose.

5.5 Financial Capital — Fuel

Finally, every vessel needs fuel. Financial capital of profit, cash flow, assets are not the goal. It is the energy that powers the mission. Treated rightly, it multiplies impact. Treated wrongly, it becomes an idol. Financial capital is a good servant and a poor master. Scripture commends honoring God with wealth and being faithful in small things (Prov. 3:9-10; Luke 16:10-11, NIV) while warning that "the borrower is slave to the lender" (Prov. 22:7, NIV).

Normatively, a business exists to create goods and services, provide meaningful work, and steward resources for the common good under God, not to maximize shareholder gain at any cost (Van Duzer, 2010). In BAM (Business as Mission), money is missional fuel. It sustains witness, enables justice in pricing and pay, and is reinvested to bless communities (Gort, 2018; Johnson, 2011). Corporate finance adds prudence. Leverage increases expected return and risk. Resilient companies guard liquidity, match asset and liability durations, and maintain a margin of safety (Brealey, Myers, & Allen, 2020). Together, these lenses yield a rule of life for money. Profit is necessary but not ultimate. Cash is oxygen, not an idol; debt is a tool, not a savior. Capital structure, working-capital discipline, and investment pacing are therefore acts of stewardship and mission, aligning financial decisions with the enterprise's Kingdom purpose (Johnson, 2011; Van Duzer, 2010).

During the Midwest farm crisis of the 1980s in America, Donald expanded aggressively. When prices collapsed, his lender pulled credit, and he lost the family land twice. Friends helped him renegotiate, rent back acreage, and rebuild. Years later, he regained solvency, upgraded to GPS-enabled equipment, and resumed multigenerational farming. Donald's sober testimony captures the spiritual and financial truth. "Debt could be a leverage or a killer. Faith could save one's life" (Ma, 2024, p. 121). His story embodies biblical cautions about enslavement to debt (Prov. 22:7, NIV) and corporate-finance basics that leverage amplifies both outcomes and fragility (Brealey et al., 2020). Yet the turning point was communal grace when advocates stood with him and he had persistent faith that God "will bring the right people in my path" (Ma, 2024, p. 121). Stewardship here meant right-sizing the balance sheet, pacing growth, and letting profit serve people and land rather than rule them (Van Duzer, 2010).

Thomas operates a small community farm while serving as a USDA scientist and professor. His journey from Mormon to Quaker faith shapes his pursuit of seed diversity and land care, privileging modest scale and ecological soundness over rapid expansion (Ma, 2024). His capital posture is patient and values-constrained in that he invested slowly, avoided burdensome debt, and let mission determine money. By contrast, Brian, a farmer-accountant, learned cash discipline during the 1980s crisis. He used financial expertise to help his father navigate distress, then sustained a dual vocation in "farming and numbers," building resilience through conservative leverage and careful cash-flow planning (Ma, 2024, p. 109). Together, their choices illustrate a shared theology of stewardship expressed through different financial strategies. Thomas emphasizes creation care and sufficiency, whereas Brian emphasizes liquidity, pacing sales, and protecting the farm's going concern, each aligning capital with vocation and the community (Johnson, 2011; Van Duzer, 2010).

These narratives affirm an important Kingdom axiom: Capital must serve calling. When faith shapes risk, pace, and liquidity, financial capital becomes the fuel that propels the vessel forward without capsizing it, honoring God, safeguarding people, and strengthening witness (Gort, 2018; Brealey etal., 2020).

In the next section "The Vessel in Motion," we integrate all four capitals—spiritual rudder, social adhesive, intellectual engine, and financial fuel—into one seaworthy craft aimed at the glory of God and the flourishing of neighbors.

5.6 The Vessel in Motion

Kingdom enterprise is not a docked idea but a vessel underway. With spiritual capital as the rudder, we steer by worship, Scripture, and prayerful discernment. "Seek first his kingdom and his righteousness" (Matt. 6:33, NIV). Social capital is the rigging and hull, with relationships of trust, reciprocity, and forgiveness that hold under strain (cf. Sorenson & Milbrandt, 2023). Intellectual capital is the engine, with creativity, insight, and systems that convert wisdom into design (Bratianu, 2025; Marr, 2018). Financial capital is the fuel. Cash, profit, assets, and prudent leverage that enable distance without defining destination (Van Duzer, 2010). The Common Good Treasure (CGT) is this balanced and dynamic equilibrium.

Flourishing comes not by maximizing a single capital but by continually shaping all four for Kingdom course and Common-Good seas (Ma, 2024). Whatever the task, we "work at it with all [our] heart, as working for the Lord" (Col. 3:23–24, NIV).

Across our field stories, the vessels moved forward. Elizabeth Tailor practiced "slow work" and dignity in craft as a witness; David & Barbara Flower Farm prayed their rows into hospitality; Joseph Medinformatics harnessed data stewardship for healing; William Conservation Farm designed whole-farm systems for soil and neighbors; Donald Kevin Jason Family Farm treated debt as a tool, not a master; Thomas Community Farm and Brian Family Farm weathered lean seasons with shared wisdom and disciplined cash flow (Ma, 2024). In each case, spiritual bearings shaped social trust, which unlocked learning and disciplined finance. The CGT is in motion!

Thus, the call is simple yet demanding. Keep the rudder true (daily surrender), the hull sound (peacemaking and fairness), the engine tuned (lifelong learning and thoughtful design), and the tanks managed (profit with purpose and patient capital). Led by the Spirit at the helm, enterprises can sail toward shalom—God's glory and the neighbors' good—in their specific waters (Ma, 2024; Van Duzer, 2010). The vessel is ready. The map is clear. The wind is at your back. Now the question is: **Will you set sail?**

We now move from metaphor to management. Chapter 6 introduces The Common Good Treasure Assessment (CGTA), a practical diagnostic tool to "visualize" your vessel across the four capitals, identify imbalances, and chart concrete next steps for Kingdom-aligned performance (Ma, 2024).

6
MEASURING
THE COMMON GOOD TREASURE

6. MEASURING THE COMMON GOOD TREASURE

6.1 From Concept to Measurement

A ship without navigational instruments may have a strong hull and an experienced crew, but it will eventually drift off course. The same is true for businesses. Without a reliable way to measure alignment with God's purposes, even the best-intentioned leaders risk losing their Kingdom direction.

The Common Good Treasure (CGT) describes the integrated spiritual, social, intellectual, and financial capital God entrusts to a business for His glory and the community's flourishing (Ma, 2024). To steward this vessel well, leaders need a way to "test everything" and pursue what is best (1 Thess. 5:21, NIV). The Common Good Treasure Assessment (CGTA) turns insight into practice. It translates the CGT into observable domains, enables baseline and growth tracking, and provides a dashboard for leaders to pray over, discuss, and improve together. The assessment is formative rather than punitive. It offers a compass for efficient and effective navigation.

CGTA also reflects the best of the holistic vision of business as ministry. Business viability is married to spiritual and social transformation, not as competing goals but as one calling (Lausanne Occasional Paper 59, 2004). It honors what my fieldwork discovered in the U.S. rural Midwest firms, especially the interplay of wisdom, trust, know-how, and cash as a single, living system (Ma, 2024). It further resonates with research on faith-based enterprises. Family faith and values shape durable social capital; embedded Christian identity legitimizes entrepreneurial action; and kingdom-minded culture sustains integrity over time (Sorenson & Milbrandt, 2023; Clark, 2021; Sangwa & Mutabazi, 2025).

This chapter introduces the **CGTA framework**—a tool designed to help you measure what matters most in business as ministry, so your vessel can sail with confidence toward the common good for the glory of God.

6.2 Why We Need the CGTA

Imagine two very different companies:

Business A (Profitable Drift): A tech startup achieving financial success. Yet spiritual capital was ignored, the culture grew toxic, and lawsuits soon followed.
Business B (Righteous Stagnation): A mission-driven coffee shop served its community with passion but neglected financial and intellectual capital. After two years, it was nearly bankrupt.

What these businesses lack is not desire, but measurement. Without an instrument like CGTA, one drifted from righteousness while the other stalled despite good intentions. Leaders can often sense imbalance. A company may run with impressive cash discipline yet lack trust, or brim with passion yet lack systems that turn insight into sustainable value. CGTA surfaces those asymmetries early. It offers (1) a **common language** for boardroom, shop floor, and church partners; (2) a **replicable measure** to evaluate practices against the CGT; and (3) a **team process** that strengthens shared discernment and ownership. In short, it connects theology, missiology, and management through what we believe (kingdom purpose), whom we serve (neighbors near and far), and how we operate (excellent, ethical, fruitful).

The CGTA framework brings balance. It helps businesses understand where they are, why they are stuck, and how to realign all capital—spiritual, social, intellectual, and financial—for Kingdom flourishing.

6.3 The CGTA Framework

CGTA is built on the **Vessel Framework** established in Chapter 5. It measures four interrelated domains:

Spiritual Capital – The Rudder

Spiritual capital is the compass that aligns a business with God's purposes. It encompasses wisdom, values, culture, and ministry. It reflects a Godward orientation (Ma, 2024).

Social Capital – The Adhesive

Social capital consists of relationships, trust, goodwill, and cooperation (Ma, 2024). It binds owners, employees, families, and the community in durable relationships (Sorenson & Milbrandt, 2023).

Intellectual Capital – The Engine

Intellectual capital includes creativity, insight, brand, and systems. It is the engine that propels the ship forward (Ma, 2024). It converts insight into value at scale (Sangwa & Mutabazi, 2025).

Financial Capital – The Fuel

Financial capital—profit, cash, debt, and assets—is the fuel that sustains missions without idolatry (Ma, 2024).

Figure 10. The Common Good Treasure - CGT

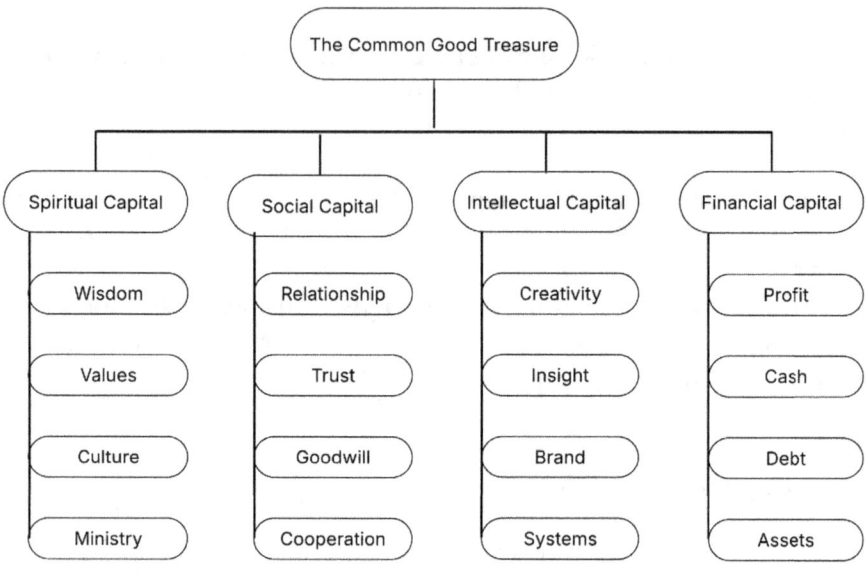

When these four capitals align, businesses operate as vessels for the Kingdom, carrying the **common good treasure** for the glory of God.

Since CGTA is formative, each domain is scored independently (to respect different growth paths) and also visualized together (to notice the imbalance that can capsize the vessel).

A four-axis radar chart displays the four capitals—Rudder (Spiritual), Adhesive (Social), Engine (Intellectual), and Fuel (Financial)—on a 1–5 scale. The dotted band (3.5–4.5) marks the balanced zone, and the outer ring holds testimonies and notes.

Figure 11. The Vessel – CGTA

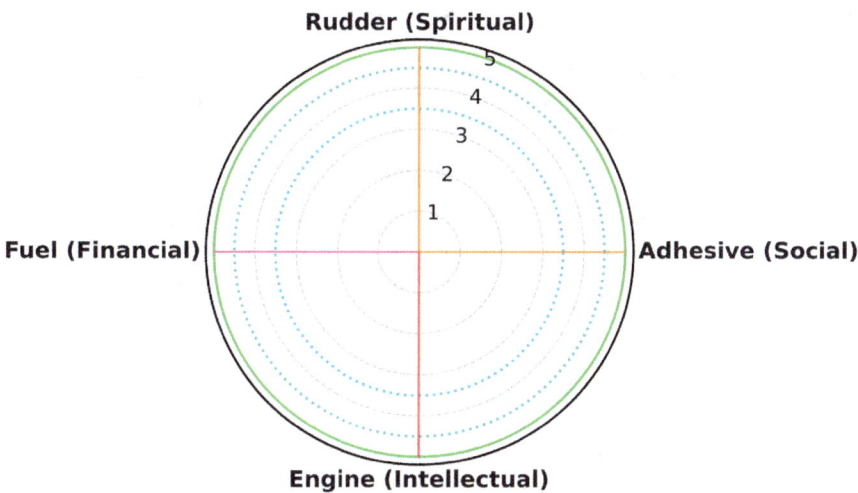

6.4 The CGTA Items and Scoring

The CGTA comprises 16 items (4 per domain), each scored on a 5-point Likert scale (1 = Not at all true · 2 = Rarely true · 3 = Sometimes true · 4 = Often true · 5 = Consistently true). Compute each domain as the **mean** of its four items. The overall CGTA is the simple average of the four domain means. Use team medians and interquartile ranges to surface alignment or misalignment.

CGTA can be administered (a) individually to leaders and key staff; (b) as a team with facilitated dialogue; and (c) longitudinally (e.g., quarterly) to track changes. Use the CGTA Radar Chart to visualize each administration.

Table 1. CGTA

Domain	Code	Item stem (last 90 days)	Reverse?	Evidence prompt (optional; not scored)
Rudder (Spiritual)	Sp1	We begin significant decisions with prayerful discernment (e.g., brief Scripture, prayer, listening).		Decision notes show a prayer/Scripture moment.
	Sp2	We are proud to embrace Christian values—honoring God and serving our stakeholders—as the foundation of our organizational culture.		Christian values appear in organizational vision and mission statements, agendas, plans, and reviews.
	Sp3	Our ethics (truthfulness, justice, mercy, stewardship) shape hiring, pricing, and supplier choices.		A recent decision shows ethics over convenience.
	Sp4	Faith practices have little to do with how we communicate, plan, hire, or serve.	R	Minutes show no spiritual framing.
Adhesive (Social)	So1	Teams help one another succeed; collaboration across roles is normal.		Cross team projects completed.
	So2	We run listening loops with employees/customers/suppliers and act on what we heard.		One ask→act→announce cycle completed.
	So3	Gossip, blame, or unresolved conflict regularly undermine trust.	R	Grievance log/pulse survey notes.
	So4	We use fair processes for people-affecting decisions (clear criteria, consistency, voice).		Process docs, appeals handled.

MEASURING THE COMMON GOOD TREASURE   69

Domain	Code	Item stem (last 90 days)	Reverse?	Evidence prompt (optional; not scored)
Engine (Intellectual)	In1	Critical know-how (SOPs, contacts, methods) is documented and accessible.		SOP library, onboarding packet updated.
	In2	We experiment and learn, improving after successes and failures.		One after action review completed.
	In3	New ideas are discouraged, or met with defensiveness.	R	Idea pipeline shows bottlenecks.
	In4	Our brand/story accurately express our purpose and the value we deliver.		Web/proposals/signage match practice.
Fuel (Financial)	Fi1	We operate with healthy margin and cash to reinvest and sustain mission.		Cash runway days, profit reinvested.
	Fi2	We use debt without a clear plan or risk thresholds.	R	Missing repayment plan/covenant watch.
	Fi3	We balance owner returns with fair wages, investment, and generosity.		Documented wage/price/giving reviews.
	Fi4	Financial reporting is timely, accurate, and understandable beyond the finance team.		Monthly one-page finance brief.

CGTA summarizes your recent pattern of practice across four capitals that together form your Common Good Treasure. Rudder (Spiritual) reflects prayerful discernment, values, and ethics that shape day-to-day decisions. Adhesive (Social) reflects trust, collaboration, listening loops, and fair people processes that hold relationships together. Engine (Intellectual) reflects documented know-how, learning from wins and losses, and disciplined problem-solving. Fuel (Financial) reflects margin and cash health, balanced returns and generosity, and timely, truthful reporting. Items focus on the last 90 days, and some are reversely scored, so higher domain scores usually signal healthier, more consistent habits. On the radar chart in Figure 12, a wider, more even shape suggests balanced stewardship, while sharp dips highlight the capital most likely constraining your current sea and your next one-cell move. Use the evidence prompts of Table 1 to confirm each score with concrete examples before setting goals or taking action.

Figure 12. CGTA Radar Chart

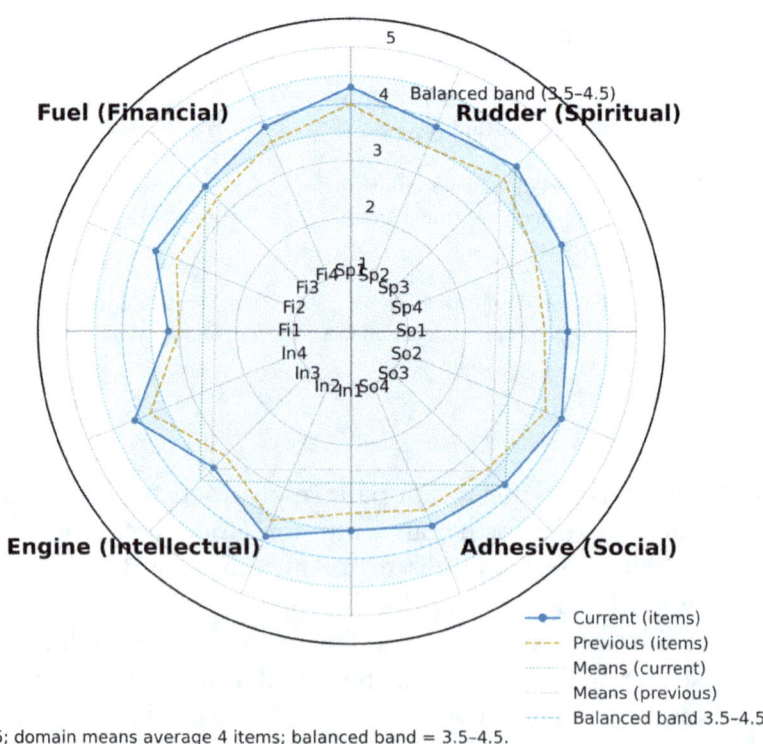

Scale 1-5; domain means average 4 items; balanced band = 3.5-4.5.

6.5 Interpreting Your CGTA Profile

Balanced Vessel with Kingdom-Flourishing Alignment: All four domains between 3.5 and 4.5, with tight team consensus. Rundle and Lee (2022) described organizations in the mission field with this profile shape as "BAMers," as illustrated in Figure 13. Companies with this CGTA profile shape and size may continue cultivating rhythms and consider mentoring peer companies.

Figure 13. Balanced Vessel with Kingdom-Flourishing Alignment

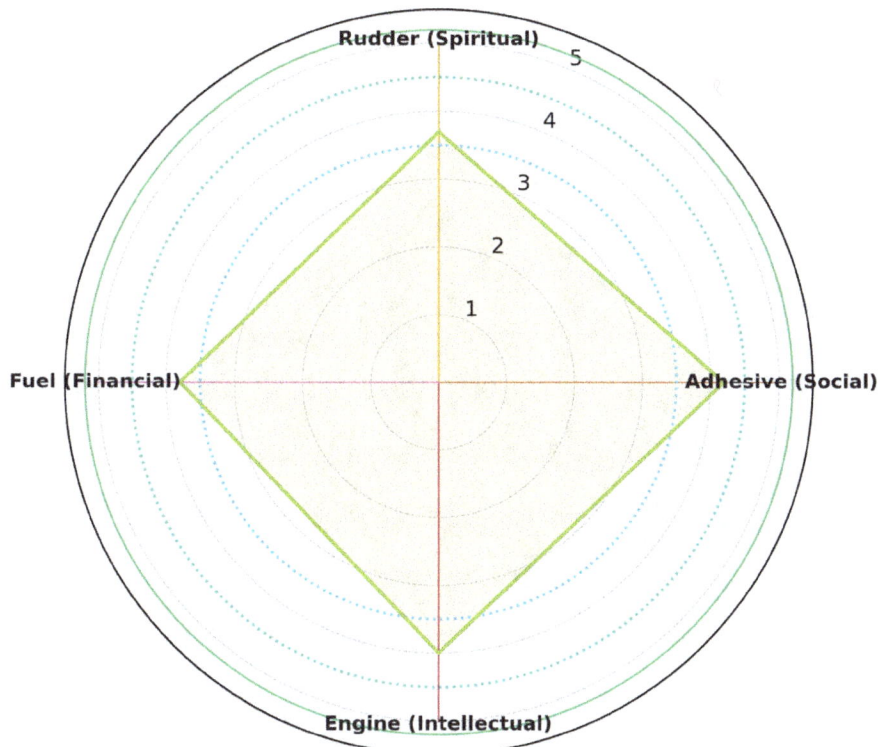

Leaning Vessel with Profitable Drift: One domain ≥1.0 point higher than the lowest (e.g., strong finance + weak trust). The stronger domain can "drag" the boat. Rundle and Lee (2022) described organizations in the mission field with this profile shape as "Faith-Driven Entrepreneurs," as visualized in Figure 14. Companies with this CGTA profile shape and size may set a 90-day plan for the low domain to restore and grow.

Figure 14. Leaning Vessel with Profitable Drift

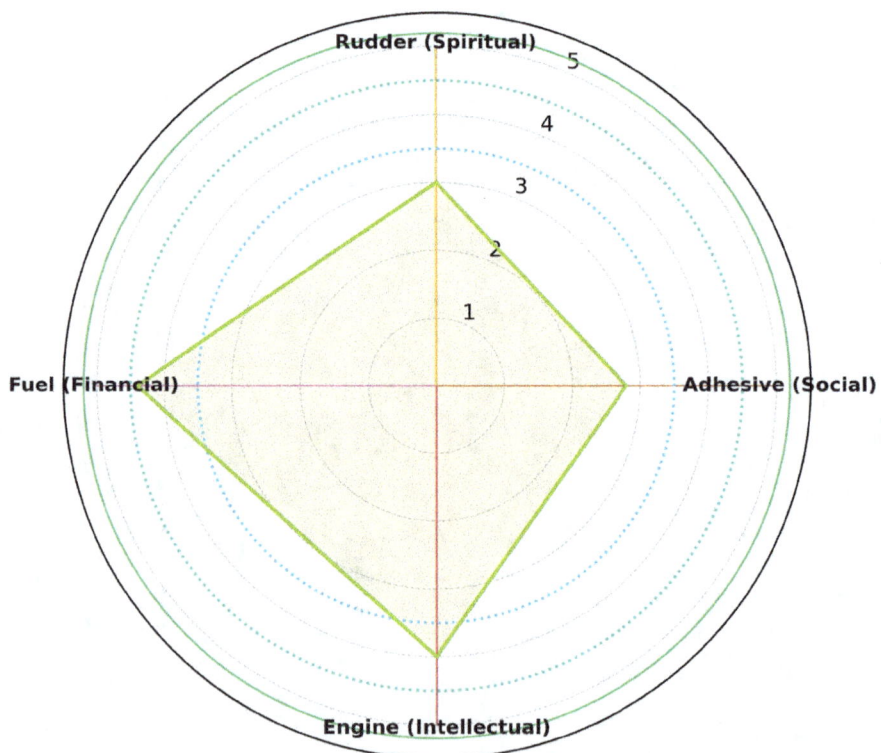

Leaking Vessel with Righteous Stagnation: Any domain <2.5. Rundle and Lee (2022) described organizations in the mission field with this profile shape as "Evangelists," as exhibited in Figure 15. Companies with this CGTA profile shape and size may halt expansion to fix the leak (e.g., toxic conflict, opacity in books).

Figure 15. Leaking Vessel with Righteous Stagnation

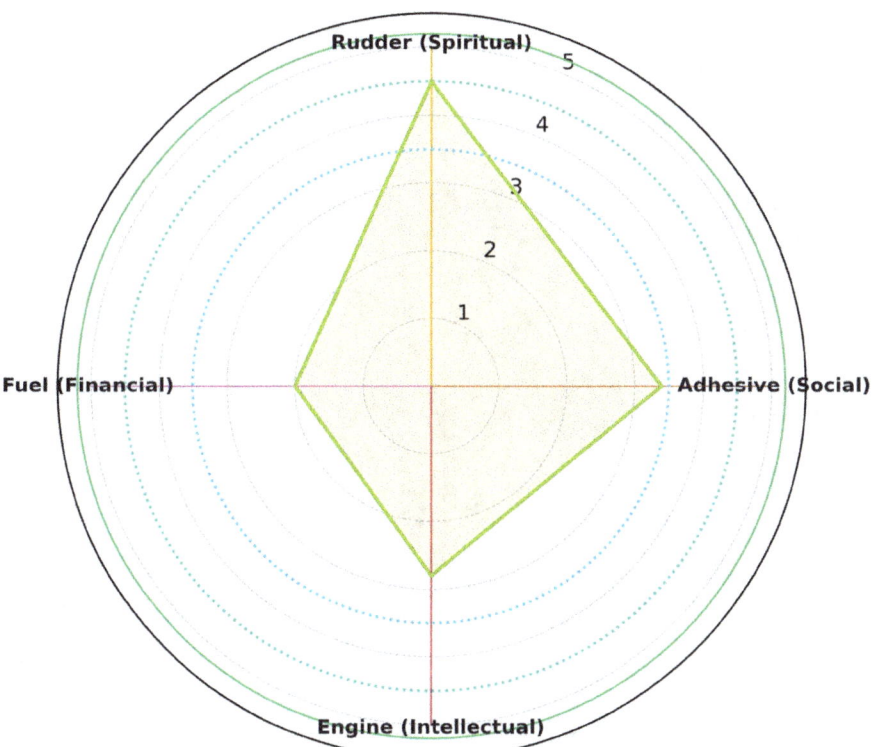

Underdeveloped Vessel as a Beginner: Overall < 3.0. Rundle and Lee (2022) described organizations in the mission field with this profile shape as "Explorers," as displayed in Figure 16. Companies with this CGTA profile shape and size may start with spiritual and social foundations and build simple systems before scaling.

Figure 16. Underdeveloped Vessel as a Beginner

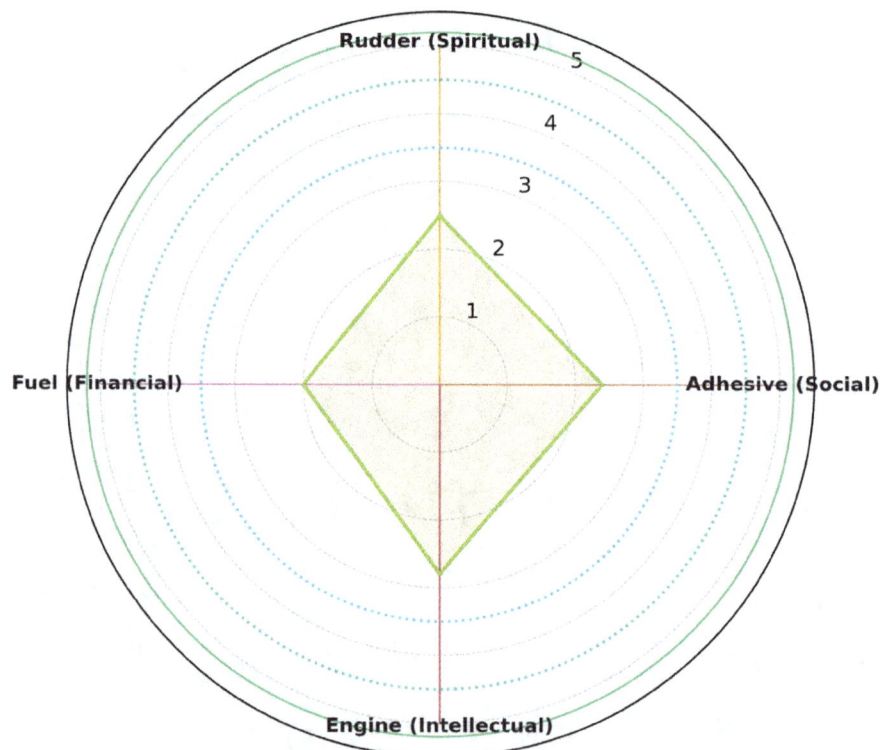

Pair scores with your own stories, e.g., prayer that brings hiring clarity (rudder), reconciliation practices after a breach (adhesive), a simple SOP that preserves quality (engine), and cash rules that survive a bad season (fuel). This would honor how values become verifiable.

6.6 Using CGTA for Growth

You may use CGTA as a quarterly "**vessel check**"personally and organizationally:

Pray and reflect (Spiritual capital): Begin with gratitude and confession, rename your stewardship before the Lord (Sangwa & Mutabazi, 2025).
Prioritize one domain for a 90-day sprint, assign an owner and two specific practices.
Share results with employees and, when appropriate, with church partners to deepen legitimacy and support (Clark, 2021).
Institutionalize learning by adding one rhythm per quarter (e.g., monthly testimony and thanks, quarterly finance open house, and biweekly Gemba for process learning).
Collaborate for the common good: use CGTA to design joint projects with local ministries and suppliers. CGTA becomes a common grammar for kingdom collaboration (Lausanne Movement, 2004).

You may run CGTA periodically to track trends, detect early signs of drift, and correct course before problems escalate.

6.7 From Score to Transformation

Measurement is never the destination. CGTA is not just a tool—it is a map for direction, a compass for continual alignment, and a call to steward every resource for the glory of God and the flourishing of His people. With CGTA, we now have a shared compass. In the next chapter, we will turn scores into practices—moving from measurement to transformation through short-cycle experiments, testimonies, and governance rhythms that keep the vessel focused on the common good for God's glory.

7

FROM SCHOLARSHIP TO PRACTICE

7. FROM SCHOLARSHIP TO PRACTICE

7.1 Using an analogy

This chapter transitions from ideas to practical application. It builds on the concepts presented in Volume 1 and offers a straightforward approach for working on Mondays in Volume 2. We envisage one central idea: **Business as Ministry** is like a **vessel** navigating **God's ocean**, which we refer to as **the 4×4 Matrix**. The rows represent the various **weather** conditions that affect markets, while the columns symbolize the underlying seabed **geology** or operational models beneath the surface. Each cell within this matrix represents a distinct **sea** with its own characteristics. Your company sails this ocean, carrying valuable **treasure**.

This treasure comprises four capitals. The **rudder** symbolizes spiritual capital, the **adhesive** represents social capital, the **engine** denotes intellectual capital, and the **fuel** stands for financial capital. Together, they form the Common Good Treasure (**CGT**), which is assessed using the Common Good Treasure Assessment (**CGTA**), serving as your **nautical chart**.

Our goal is clear: To help Christian entrepreneurs understand the market's weather patterns and underlying geology. We aim to show how to use the CGTA to locate your vessel, observe the currents, and make adjustment one faithful degree at a time. We do not repeat the content of Volume 1 in Volumes 2, 3, and 4. Instead, we apply it in a practical way. We use simple language, focus on small actions, and maintain a pastoral yet firm tone throughout. The process emphasizes seeing, praying, measuring, deciding, and doing, with the intention of repeating this cycle each quarter.

7.2 Reading the weather

Every market breathes a moral climate. This climate is the **weather** that blows across the ocean. In **Jungle** weather, trust is thin. Power is uneven. Horizons are short. People hoard information and push harm onto their neighbors. The first repair here is simple yet hard. Tell the truth. Keep one promise that helps the weak. Pay the smallest suppliers on time. Build the habit of fair process so quieter voices are heard. You will feel the wind shift when people begin to speak without fear (Benedict XVI, 2009; Smith, 1759/2000).

In **Exchange** weather courts work. Reputation matters. Deals are predictable. The risk is a cold heart. Work becomes only a contract. Here you widen accountability. Ask which stakeholders need a voice. Explain decisions. Set expectations for help during change. All this keeps exchange human (Freeman, 2010; Donaldson & Preston, 1995).

Moral Sentiment weather values dignity and conscience. People care about what is right. The risk is fatigue and performance. You connect sentiments to structures. Tie justice to pay, schedules, safety, and inclusion. Add sabbath pacing so care remains joyful and strong (Smith, 1759/2000).

Gratuitousness weather is grace. Gift and forgiveness do not replace trade. They underwrite it. Mercy becomes normal. The risk is imprudence. So, you pair generosity with clean cash and clear guardrails. Public acts of thanks and reconciliation keep grace visible without shaming those who have less to give (Benedict XVI, 2009). This weather is the best to sail in. It invites a fleet to move together for the common good.

7.3 Reading the geology

Under the water lies the **geology**, the business models. It is the basis upon which your organization navigates when circumstances change. **SWM** emphasizes the importance of managing the cost of capital, maintaining disciplined cash management, and achieving risk-adjusted returns. This approach is particularly effective in price-sensitive markets and when seeking access to capital. However, there is a risk of treating people merely as resources. Therefore, boards of directors must implement disclosures and constraints to ensure that profit serves as a means to an end, and never becomes the ultimate goal (Friedman, 2007; Jensen & Meckling, 1976; Van Duzer, 2010).

ST promotes accountability among owners, employees, customers, suppliers, and the community, thereby building trust. The challenge is transitioning from storytelling to effective governance. Ensuring access to information, providing grievance channels, setting supplier standards, and fostering open dialogue are essential to involving weaker parties in genuine decision-making. This approach transforms servant leadership into a fundamental way of operating, rather than merely a marketing slogan (Freeman, 2010; Donaldson & Preston, 1995).

CG aims for good goods, good work, and good wealth. It emphasizes subsidiarity and justice as guiding principles in decision-making. The practical task is to integrate moral objectives into budgets, supplier agreements, and compensation practices. It also requires the courage to decline profitable opportunities that harm individuals or the environment, all done with clarity and grace (Sison & Fontrodona, 2011; McVea & Naughton, 2021).

BaM integrates all four types of capital into a single, cohesive good. Servantship is essential to this approach. Leaders pray during planning, communicate honestly, repair harm when needed, and manage finances with humility. A crucial question to consider is balance: Which practices enhance one type of capital without depleting the others? It is important to learn to identify early signs of drift. Together, we can recover through confession and by implementing wise guardrails (Wong & Rae, 2011; Tan, 2006).

In summary, the foundational geology you choose significantly influences how your vessel navigates storms.

7.4 The ocean and its seas

The 4×4 Matrix is best understood as an **ocean** rather than a scoreboard. Currents flow from south to north, while seabed **geology** extends from west to east. Each intersection forms a distinct **sea** with its own moral and managerial characteristics. A vessel navigates these waters in relation to suppliers, customers, employees, churches, and communities. Four fundamental elements sustain the vessel:

Spiritual capital is the **rudder** that guides its direction under God's guidance.
Social capital serves as the **adhesive** that keeps the crew united.
Intellectual capital acts as the **engine** that transforms learning into value.
Financial capital is the **fuel** that powers the voyage.

When these elements are well-organized, the vessel can navigate smoothly. However, if any element is obstructed, the ability to steer becomes compromised (Benedict XVI, 2009; Van Duzer, 2010).

Three scholarly trajectories can be identified. First, there is the concept of **niche fit and resilience**. Some weather-geology pairings are stable, while others are fragile. We can pinpoint **keystone practices** that help stabilize a particular environment. Examples of these practices include fair decision-making processes, timely payments to even the smallest suppliers, honest safety reporting, and maintaining a balanced work pace.

Secondly, we examine **succession and migration**. Most movements occur into an adjacent sea. Mixed methods can help identify which disturbances and habits promote healthy movement and which do not (Sorenson & Milbrandt, 2023).

Lastly, we consider **feedback, thresholds, and evidence**. Small changes can significantly affect a system. For instance, eliminating a predatory term may enhance trust and accelerate learning. However, using moral language without sound financial practices can drain a system's resources. Formative measurement is essential for recognizing these effects without exaggerating them (AERA et al., 2014; Kane, 2013). As a result, the matrix becomes a navigable ocean rather than a static grid.

7.5 Reading the treasure with a chart

The vessel carries treasure, including spiritual, social, intellectual, and financial capital. Your crew needs a standardized method to assess the treasure you carry. The method is CGTA. CGTA measures the **Rudder** and **Adhesive** together as the **Kingdom Orientation Index** (**KOI**) and the **Engine** and **Fuel** together as the **Value-Creation Capacity** (**VCC**). Plotting these two numbers locates the vessel in one sea in the previous quarter. Repeating this process for the current quarter shows the movement.

Two key principles safeguard integrity. First, present numbers and stories together. For every statistic, include a personal account from someone closely involved in the work. Second, report a change only when it is genuine. A change is genuine when it has been felt for at least two weeks and is supported by a documented story. If a change has not yet occurred, plot both points and label it as "holding position." This approach to honesty fosters trust among teams and facilitates replication across organizations and regions (Kane, 2013; Wong & Rae, 2011).

7.6 The Journey of Volume 1

Volume 1 presented a cohesive story with multiple scenes. It started by discussing the Scripture on work, emphasizing that business is often viewed as a vocation that serves both God and one's neighbor in public life. The narrative then traced a path from doctrine to practical application. We learned to envision a business as a vessel navigating God's vast ocean. To describe this ocean, we created a **4x4 Matrix**. The rows represented "weathers" that shape markets, while the columns illustrated "geologies" that define operating models beneath the water. Each cell in the matrix became its own sea, characterized by distinct colors and sensations. This journey is visually represented in Figure 17, which depicts the transition from theology to practice, from literature review to empirical study, and from research to development, highlighting their integration.

Volume 1 also defined the treasures on board. Spiritual capital serves as the **rudder** that sets the direction under God. Social capital acts as the **adhesive** that holds the crew together. Intellectual capital is the **engine** that converts learning into value, while financial capital functions as the **fuel** that powers the voyage. Together, they form what we call the Common Good Treasure (**CGT**).

We then introduced a nautical chart to carefully navigate this treasure. The Common Good Treasure Assessment (**CGTA**) provides two coordinates—Key Operational Indicators (KOI) and Value

Creation Capacity (VCC)—to help locate the vessel and measure progress through both numbers and stories. Measurement serves people, not the other way around (AERA et al., 2014; Kane, 2013).

The journey concludes with a simple yet profound reminder: Move one step at a time. Keep prayer, prudence, and maintenance in mind. Let your work become an act of worship in the business ocean (Benedict XVI, 2009; Van Duzer, 2010).

Figure 17. The journey of Volume 1

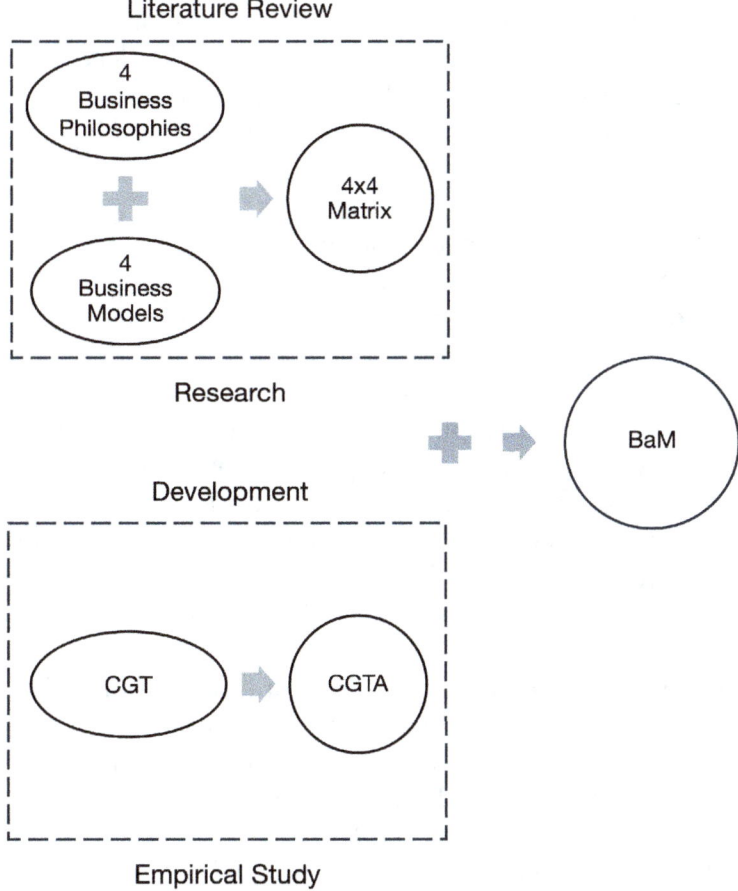

7.7 The Framework of Volumes 1, 2, 3, and 4

The four-volume project has now been integrated into a cohesive framework comprising four distinct components. Figure 18 shows how each book occupies its own space while reinforcing the others.

Volume 1 establishes the "why." It defines the ocean, weather, geology, seas, treasures, and charts, providing readers with a precise map, common definitions, and a replicable method.

Volume 2 focuses on the "how" and applies these concepts to weekly life. It maintains the same maritime framework, helping teams understand and act accordingly. This volume teaches leaders to pray briefly, read the CGT, complete the CGTA, select one keystone practice, and hold a fifteen-minute meeting every Monday.

Volume 3 serves as the practice workbook. It contains tiered exercises and guidance for facilitators, enabling companies, churches, peer groups, and classrooms to engage collectively in this journey.

Volume 4 is the devotional prayerbook. It invites leaders and teams to devote the entire voyage—its people, its treasure, its decisions—back to God through Scripture, prayer, confession, and worship. Together, these four components form a unified force, steering a collective toward the Spring Green Shalom Sea.

This framework also serves as a research program. Volume 1 provides constructs and tools that scholars and practitioners can use across regions and sectors. Volume 2 generates field evidence that can be coded and compared for analysis. Volume 3 fosters a community of practice that shares data and narratives. Volume 4 sustains the spiritual posture that keeps the research and practice accountable to God and neighbor. Together, these volumes share a unified moral purpose: To measure in ways that respect individuals, publish in ways that build trust, and guide actions that enhance both **Kingdom orientation** and **value creation**. This requires persistent effort rather than a quick sprint. It requires both humility and courage. The focus is on the public good rather than personal recognition. It keeps the vessel moving in the right direction even when winds shift (Freeman, 2010; Smith, 2000; Wong & Rae, 2011).

Figure 18. The framework of Volumes 1, 2, 3, and 4

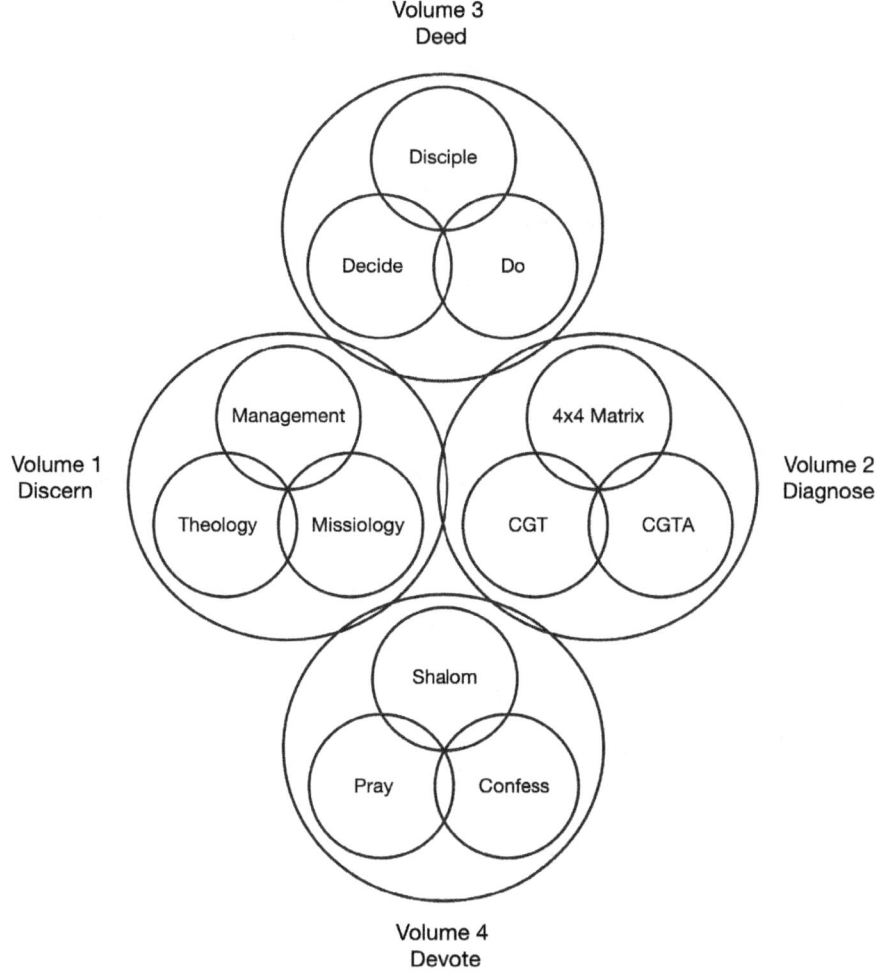

REFERENCES

AERA, APA, & NCME. (2014). *THE STANDARDS FOR EDUCATIONAL AND PSYCHOLOGICAL TESTING*. American Educational Research Association. https://www.testingstandards.net/

Benedict XVI. (2009). *Caritas in veritate (June 29, 2009) | BENEDICT XVI*. https://www.vatican.va/content/benedict-xvi/en/encyclicals/documents/hf_ben-xvi_enc_20090629_caritas-in-veritate.html#_edn8

Bratianu, C. (2025). A Complexity Framework for Understanding Intellectual Capital. In A. Kianto, S. Čabrilo, & L. Užienė (Eds.), *Futurizing Intellectual Capital: Insights on Navigating Knowledge-Based Value Creation* (pp. 9–27). Springer Nature Switzerland. https://doi.org/10.1007/978-3-031-80197-6_2

Brealey, R. A., Myers, S. C., & Allen, F. (2020). *Principles of Corporate Finance*. McGraw-Hill Education.

Chalmers, T. (2010). *On Natural Theology V2*. Kessinger Publishing, LLC.

Charmaz, K. (2014). *Constructing Grounded Theory* (Second edition). SAGE Publications Ltd.

Costantino, T. E. (2008). Constructivism. In *The SAGE Encyclopedia of Qualitative Research Methods* (pp. 116–119). SAGE Publications.

Creswell, J. W., & Creswell, J. D. (2018). *Research design: Qualitative, quantitative, and mixed methods approaches* (Fifth edition.). SAGE Publications, Inc.

Creswell, J. W., & Poth, C. N. (2018). *Qualitative Inquiry and Research Design: Choosing Among Five Approaches* (4th ed.). SAGE Publications.

Dawar, N. (2013). When Marketing Is Strategy. *Harvard Business Review*. https://hbr.org/2013/12/when-marketing-is-strategy

Donaldson, T., & Preston, L. E. (1995). The Stakeholder Theory of the Corporation: Concepts, Evidence, and Implications. *The Academy of Management Review, 20*(1), 65–91. https://doi.org/10.5465/AMR.1995.9503271992

D'Souza, S. (2017). Gardening as a Source of Spiritual Capital. In M. O'Sullivan & B. Flanagan (Eds.), *Spiritual Capital: Spirituality in Practice in Christian Perspective* (pp. 159–170). Routledge.

Faldetta, G. (2012). The Logic of Gift and Gratuitousness in Business Relationship. *Journal of Business Ethics, 100*, 67–77.

Felber, C., Campos, V., & Sanchis, J. R. (2019). The Common Good Balance Sheet, an Adequate Tool to Capture Non-Financials? *Sustainability, 11*(14), Article 14. https://doi.org/10.3390/su11143791

Flick, U. (2022). *Doing interview research: The essential how to guide*. Sage Publications.

Freeman, R. E. (1984). *Strategic Management: A Stakeholder Approach*. Pitman. https://www.ebay.com/itm/133770763933

Freeman, R. E. (2010). *Strategic Management: A Stakeholder Approach*. Cambridge University Press. https://doi.org/10.1017/CBO9781139192675

Freeman, R. E., & Reed, D. L. (1983). Stockholders and Stakeholders: A New Perspective on Corporate Governance. *California Management Review, 25*(3), 88–106. https://doi.org/10.2307/41165018

Friedman, M. (2007). The Social Responsibility of Business Is to Increase Its Profits. In W. C. Zimmerli, M. Holzinger, & K. Richter (Eds.), *Corporate Ethics and Corporate Governance* (pp. 173–178). Springer. https://doi.org/10.1007/978-3-540-70818-6_14

Glesne, C. (2016). *Becoming Qualitative Researchers: An Introduction, 5th Edition* (Nos. 978-0-13-385939–3; Pearson). Pearson.

Gort, G. (2018). *BAM Global Movement: Business as Mission Concepts and Stories*. Hendrickson Publishers.

Grant, R. M. (1991). The Resource-Based Theory of Competitive Advantage: Implications for Strategy Formulation. *California Management Review, 33*(3), 114–135. https://doi.org/10.2307/41166664

Greenleaf, R. K. (2013). *Servant Leadership [25th Anniversary Edition]: A Journey into the Nature of Legitimate Power and Greatness*. Paulist Press.

Guba, E. G., & Lincoln, Y. S. (2000). Competing paradigms in qualitative research. In *Handbook of qualitative research* (1st ed., pp. 105–117). SAGE.

Jensen, M. C., & Meckling, W. H. (1976). Theory of the firm: Managerial behavior, agency costs and ownership structure. *Journal of Financial Economics, 3*(4), 305–360. https://doi.org/10.1016/0304-405X(76)90026-X

Johnson, C. N. (2011). *Business as Mission: A Comprehensive Guide to Theory and Practice*. InterVarsity Press.

Kane, M. T. (2013). Validating the Interpretations and Uses of Test Scores. *Journal of Educational Measurement, 50*(1), 1–73. https://doi.org/10.1111/jedm.12000

Lausanne Movement. (2004). *Business as Mission – Lausanne Occasional Paper No. 59*. Lausanne Committee for World Evangelization. https://lausanne.org/occasional-paper/business-mission-lop-59

Lin, T. C. W. (2018). *Incorporating Social Activism* (SSRN Scholarly Paper No. 3294317). Social Science Research Network. https://papers.ssrn.com/sol3/papers.cfm?abstract_id=3294317

Lovrich, N. P., & Pierce, J. C. (2016). Social Capital and Organizational Change. In A. Farazmand (Ed.), *Global Encyclopedia of Public Administration, Public Policy, and Governance* (pp. 1–10). Springer International Publishing. https://doi.org/10.1007/978-3-319-31816-5_2352-1

Ma, E. Z. (2024). *Business as Ministry in the US Rural Midwest for the Common Good* [Doctoral Dissertation, Biola University]. https://www.proquest.com/docview/3031708223

Marr, B. (2018). Intellectual Capital. In M. Augier & D. J. Teece (Eds.), *The Palgrave Encyclopedia of Strategic Management* (pp. 772–775). Palgrave Macmillan UK. https://doi.org/10.1057/978-1-137-00772-8_317

McCann, D. (2011). The Principle of Gratuitousness: Opportunities and Challenges for Business in «Caritas in Veritate». *Journal of Business Ethics*, *100*, 55–66.

McLeod, S. (2025, August 3). *Maslow's Hierarchy of Needs*. https://www.simplypsychology.org/maslow.html

McVea, J. F., & Naughton, M. J. (2021). Enriching Social Entrepreneurship from the Perspective of Catholic Social Teaching. *Religions*, *12*(3), Article 3. https://doi.org/10.3390/rel12030173

Merriam, S. B., & Tisdell, E. J. (2016). *Qualitative research: A guide to design and implementation* (Fourth edition.). John Wiley & Sons.

Miles, M. B., Huberman, A. M., & Saldana, J. (2018). *Qualitative Data Analysis: A Methods Sourcebook*. SAGE Publications.

Novak, M. (1990). *Toward a theology of the corporation* (Rev. ed.). AEI Press.

O'Brien, W. (2017). Spiritual Capital in a Competitive Workplace. In M. O'Sullivan & B. Flanagan (Eds.), *Spiritual Capital: Spirituality in Practice in Christian Perspective* (pp. 97–109). Routledge.

Phillips, R., Barney, J., Freeman, R. E., & Harrison, J. (2019). Stakeholder Theory. In J. Harrison, J. Barney, R. E. Freeman, & R. Phillips (Eds.), *The Cambridge handbook of stakeholder theory*. Cambridge University Press.

Rieger, J. (2015). Reconfigurating the Common Good and Religion in the Context of Capitalism: Abrahamic Alternative. In M. Johnson-DeBaufre (Ed.), *Common goods: Economy, ecology, and political theology / Melanie Johnson-DeBaufre, Catherine Keller, and Elias Ortega-Aponte, editors.* (First edition..). Fordham University Press.

Rourke, T. R. (1996). Michael Novak and Yves R. Simon on the Common Good and Capitalism. *The Review of Politics*, *58*(2), 229–258. https://doi.org/10.1017/S0034670500019355

Saldaña, J. (2021). *The Coding Manual for Qualitative Researchers*. SAGE.

Schwandt, T. A. (2015). *The SAGE dictionary of qualitative inquiry* (Fourth edition.). SAGE.

Shafique, I., Rafi, N., & Kalyar, M. N. (2021). Managing Intellectual Capital Through Strategic Leadership: A Complementary Approach. In M. Shahbaz, M. S. Mubarik, & T. Mahmood (Eds.), *The Dynamics of Intellectual Capital in Current Era* (pp. 257–274). Springer. https://doi.org/10.1007/978-981-16-1692-1_13

Shenton, A. K. (2004). Strategies for Ensuring Trustworthiness in Qualitative Research Projects. *Education for Information*, *22*(2), 63–75.

Sison, A. J. G., & Fontrodona, J. (2011). The Common Good of Business: Addressing a

Challenge Posed by «Caritas in Veritate». *Journal of Business Ethics, 100*(1), 99–107. https://doi.org/10.1007/s10551-011-1181-6

Sison, A. J. G., & Fontrodona, J. (2013). Participating in the Common Good of the Firm. *Journal of Business Ethics, 113*(4), 611–625. https://doi.org/10.1007/s10551-013-1684-4

Smith, A. (1759). *The Theory of Moral Sentiments*. Liberty Fund. https://about.libertyfund.org/books/the-theory-of-moral-sentiments/

Sorenson, R. L., & Milbrandt, J. M. (2023). Family Social Capital in Family Business: A Faith-Based Values Theory. *Journal of Business Ethics, 184*(3), 701–724. https://doi.org/10.1007/s10551-022-05110-4

Sundaram, A., & Inkpen, A. (2004). The Corporate Objective Revisited. *Organization Science, 15*(3), 350–363. https://doi.org/10.1287/orsc.1040.0068

Tan, S.-Y. (2006). *Full Service: Moving from Self-Serve Christianity to Total Servanthood*. Baker Publishing Group.

Tong, J. K. C., & Yang, F. (2016). Trust at Work: A Study on Faith and Trust of Protestant Entrepreneurs in China. *Religions, 7*(12), 136. https://doi.org/10.3390/rel7120136

Turnbull, R. (2020). A Protestant View of the Common Good. *Journal of Catholic Social Thought, 17*(1), 119–138. https://doi.org/10.5840/jcathsoc20201719

Van Duzer, J. B. (2010). *Why business matters to God: (And what still needs to be fixed)*. IVP Academic.

Windsor, D. (2010). Shareholder Wealth Maximization. In J. R. Boatright (Ed.), *Finance Ethics: Critical issues in theory and practice* (pp. 435–455). John Wiley & Sons, Ltd. https://doi.org/10.1002/9781118266298.ch23

Wong, K. L., & Rae, S. B. (2011). *Business for the Common Good: A Christian Vision for the Marketplace*. InterVarsity Press.

Wookey, C., Alford, H., & Hickey, L. (2023). Advancing the Common Good Through Purpose-led Business: Catholic Social Teaching and a Blueprint for Better Business. *The Review of Faith & International Affairs, 21*(1), 53–65. https://doi.org/10.1080/15570274.2023.2177456

Wright, C. J. H. (2006). *The Mission of God: Unlocking the Bible's Grand Narrative*. IVP Academic.

Wright, C. J. H. (2025). *The Mission of God: Unlocking the Bible's Grand Narrative*. IVP Academic.

Yahanpath, N., & Joseph, T. (2011). A brief review of the role of shareholder wealth maximisation and other factors contributing to the global financial crisis. *Qualitative Research in Financial Markets, 3*(1), 64–77. https://doi.org/10.1108/17554171111124621

Zohar, D., & Marshall, I. (2011). *Spiritual Capital: Wealth We Can Live By*. A&C Black.

APPENDICES

APPENDIX A. GLOSSARY OF KEY TERMS

Business as Ministry (BaM)
A theological and missiological claim that the ordinary operations of a company can be public witness ordered to love of God and neighbor, not a philanthropy add-on or proselytizing quota (Wright, 2006/2025; Benedict XVI, 2009; Van Duzer, 2010; Sorenson & Milbrandt, 2023; Wookey, 2023; Ma, 2024).

Common Good (CG)
The network of conditions that enables persons and communities to flourish; operationalized in business as good goods, good work, and good wealth (Benedict XVI, 2009; Wong & Rae, 2011; McVea & Naughton, 2021; Wookey, 2023).

The Common Good Treasure (CGT)
A four-capital framework—Spiritual (SP), Social (SO), Intellectual (IN), and Financial (FI) capital—for describing how companies steward formation toward the common good (Ma, 2024).

The Common Good Treasure Assessment (CGTA)
A formative instrument aligned to CGT that summarizes domain means (SP, SO, IN, FI) and visualizes them on a radar chart with an interpretive band, not for ranking but flourishing (AERA et al., 2014; Kane, 2013; Ma, 2024).

Four Models
Shareholder Wealth Maximization (SWM), Stakeholder Theory (ST), Common Good (CG), and Business as Ministry (BaM) as a theological model; each has distinctive normative and instrumental claims (Jensen & Meckling, 1976; Novak, 1990; Donaldson & Preston, 1995; Rourke, 1996; Windsor, 2010; Freeman, 2010; Van Duzer, 2010; Sison & Fontrodona, 2011; Rieger, 2015; Felber, 2019; Wookey, 2023; Ma, 2024; Wright, 2025).

Four Philosophies
Jungle (power/self-protection), Exchange (contract/price), Moral Sentiments (virtue/trust), and Gratuitousness (gift/grace), used to interpret model dynamics (Smith, 1759/2004; Benedict XVI, 2009; McCann, 2011; Faldetta, 2012; McVea & Naughton, 2021).

Servantship
A posture of service that precedes and shapes leadership, emphasizes formation and fair process (Greenleaf, 2013; Tan, 2006).

RAEF
Mnemonic for the four capitals: Rudder (SP), Adhesive (SO), Engine (IN), Fuel (FI).

APPENDIX B. SCRIPTURE INDEX & THEOLOGICAL NOTES

This index anchors key biblical citations (NIV, 2011) and briefly explains how each text is used in the argument.

Table 2. Scripture Index and Theological Notes

Text (NIV, 2011)	How it is used in this volume
Genesis 1:26–28	Creation mandate, human vocation, and delegated stewardship → grounds for work and creativity.
Genesis 2:15	Cultivate and keep → meaningful work as care for creation.
Exodus 20:8–11	Sabbath → rhythm that dignifies workers and limits production idolatry.
Deuteronomy 8:10–18	Wealth and remembrance → humility and covenantal accountability in prosperity.
Psalm 24:1	The earth is the Lord's → ownership and stewardship framingfor assets and profit.
Proverbs 11:1	Honest scales → just exchange, pricing ethics.
Micah 6:8	Justice, mercy, humility → diagnostic triad for governance.
Matthew 5–7	Sermon on the Mount → virtue formation; non-anxious economics.
Matthew 25:14–30	Talents → faithful risk and accountability for entrustedresources.
Luke 10:25–37	Good Samaritan → neighbor-regarding supply chains and service.
Acts 2:42–47	Community sharing → social capital and generosity practices.
Ephesians 2:10	Workmanship and good works → vocation and prepared paths.
Colossians 3:23	Work as unto the Lord → worshipful posture in operations.

Hermeneutical note: We read these texts canonically within creation–fall–redemption–new creation and apply them to corporate practices through virtue ethics and the common good.

APPENDIX C. CGTA TECHNICAL MANUAL

Purpose and intended use:
The Common Good Treasure Assessment (CGTA) is a formative instrument designed to guide stewardship and reflection. It is not a summative ranking tool (AERA et al., 2014). Construct definition: CGT comprises four capitals (SP, SO, IN, FI) that describe formation toward the common good.

Population and setting:
Companies and organizational units; research samples should report sector, size, geography, and model context (SWM/ST/CG/BaM).
Administration: 16 items on a 1–5 Likert scale; optional free-text prompts for 'scores + stories.'

Scoring:
Reverse-score designated items; compute domain means and display a radar with a balanced band (3.5–4.5).

Reliability & validity evidence:
Content and response-process documentation; internal structure checks (domain coherence); relations to other variables (e.g., retention, NPS) interpreted cautiously (Kane, 2013).

Consequences of use:
Report formative actions taken; avoid punitive use or simplistic benchmarking (AERA et al., 2014).

Reporting standards:
Include purpose, construct map, item table, scoring rules, cautions, and a brief equity/justice note about use.

APPENDIX D. CGTA INSTRUMENTS

Item stems are organized by domain. Reverse-scored items are marked (R). Respondents select 1–5 (1 = Not at all true · 2 = Rarely true · 3 = Sometimes true · 4 = Often true · 5 = Consistently true).

Spiritual (SP) — Rudder
SP1. We begin significant decisions with prayerful discernment (e.g., brief Scripture, prayer, and listening).
SP2. We are proud to embrace Christian values—honoring God and serving our stakeholders—as the foundation of our organizational culture.
SP3. Our ethics (truthfulness, justice, mercy, stewardship) shape hiring, pricing, and supplier choices.
SP4. Faith practices have little to do with how we communicate, plan, hire, or serve. (R)

Social (SO) — Adhesive
SO1. Teams help one another succeed; collaboration across roles is normal.
SO2. We run listening loops with employees/customers/suppliers and act on what we have heard.
SO3. Gossip, blame, or unresolved conflict regularly undermine trust. (R)
SO4. We use fair processes for people-affecting decisions (clear criteria, consistency, voice).

Intellectual (IN) — Engine
IN1. The critical know-hows (SOPs, contacts, methods) are documented and accessible.
IN2. We experiment and learn, improving after successes and failures.
IN3. New ideas are discouraged or met with defensiveness. (R)
IN4. Our brand and stories accurately express our purpose and the value we deliver.

Financial (FI) — Fuel
FI1. We operate with healthy margins and cash to reinvest and sustain missions.
FI2. We use debt without a clear plan or risk thresholds. (R)
FI3. We balance owner returns with fair wages, investment, and generosity.
FI4. Financial reporting is timely, accurate, and understandable beyond the finance team.

Scoring worksheet (overview): Reverse SP4, SO3, IN3, FI2 (score 1 as 5, 2 as 4, and 3 stays as 3). Compute each domain mean (average of four items). Visualize means on a 1–5 radar with a dotted 'balanced band' between 3.5 and 4.5.

APPENDIX E. CASE STUDIES

Cases are anonymized and designed for classroom and research citation.

Case 1: An Agricultural Enterprise, Anonymized.
A 120-employee agricultural services firm navigated consolidation pressures after a drought year. Initial 'hot' practices (supplier squeeze, deferred wages) moved to an Exchange-level wage floor and transparent payables policy. Over two seasons, Moral-Sentiments practices emerged: fair-process scheduling, a hardship fund, and reconciliation circles after a safety incident. CGTA means rose from SP 3.0 / SO 3.1 / IN 3.2 / FI 3.4 to SP 3.7 / SO 3.8 / IN 3.6 / FI 3.6, represented by the green area in Figure 19. The 'one-cell move' pedagogy aided board conversations about cash as servant, not master, and reset supplier relations.

Result with weighted KOI and VCC averages: A movement within the **cell (3,3)** (row 3 × column 3) while trending toward the green (4,4), as illustrated in Figure 20. Calculations and interpretations are provided in BaM Volume 2 — Shaping a Godly Business: A BaM Monday Companion.

Figure 19. The CGT Movement of the Agricultural Enterprise

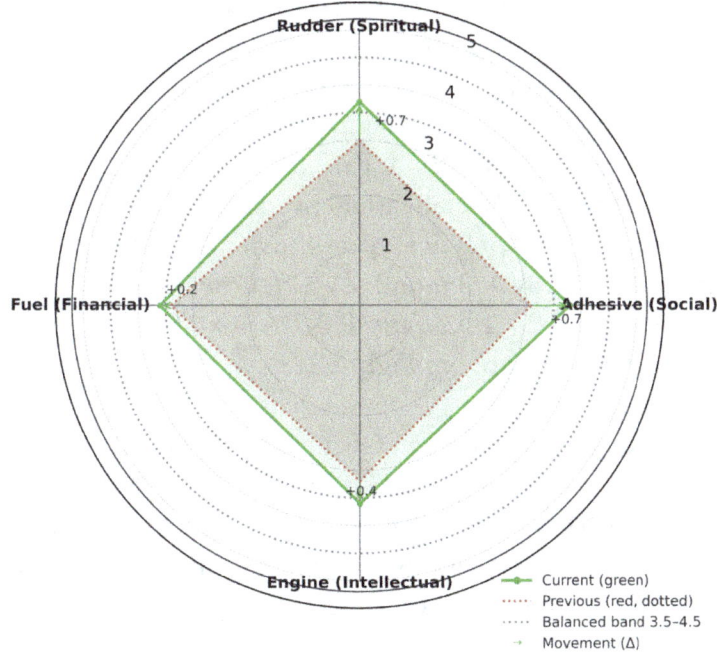

Figure 20. The Movement of the Agricultural Enterprise on the 4x4 Matrix

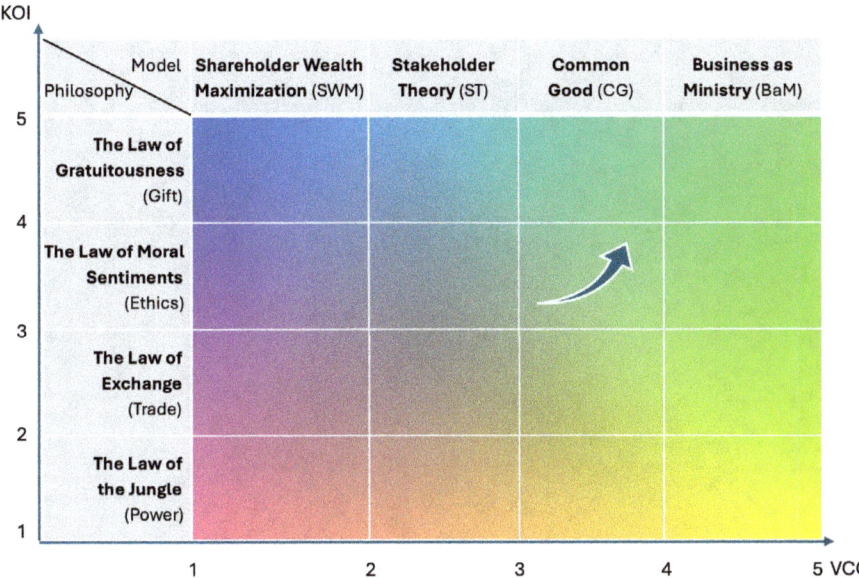

Case 2: A Health Informatics, Anonymized

A 40-person analytics firm serving hospitals faced misaligned incentives in per-bed optimization. BaM framing clarified the firm's vocation ('serve healing, not throughput'). They re-scoped a product that penalized discharges without care transitions, absorbing short-term margin loss. Social-capital practices (client listening loops) and intellectual-capital practices (post-mortems, SOPs) matured. FI guardrails kept runway > 9 months. CGTA means rose from SP 3.0 / SO 3.1 / IN 3.2 / FI 3.4 to SP 3.7 / SO 3.8 / IN 3.6 / FI 3.6, indicated by the green area in Figure 21.

Result with weighted KOI and VCC averages: Movement from **cell (2,3)** (row 2 × column 3) to **cell (3,4)** (row 3 × column 4)—a moderate diagonal one-cell improvement, as visualized in Figure 22. Calculations and interpretations are provided in BaM Volume 2 — Shaping a Godly Business: A BaM Monday Companion.

Figure 21. The CGT Movement of the Health Informatics

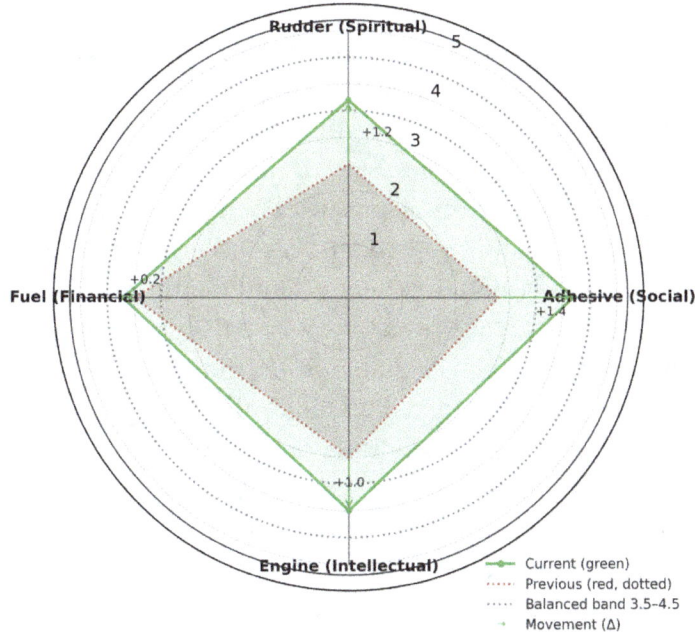

Figure 22. The Movement of the Health Informatics on the 4x4 Matrix

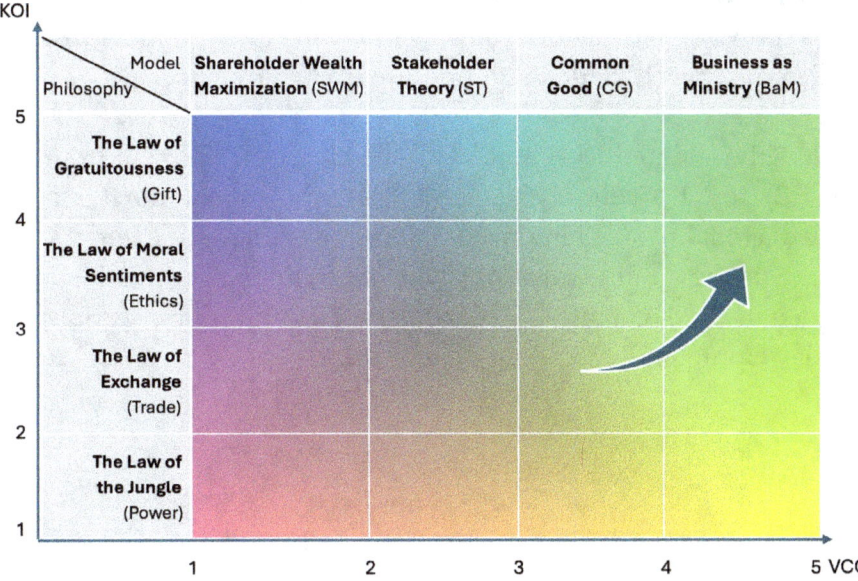

Case 3: A Textile Manufacturer, Anonymized

Small-batch apparel subcontractor with ~85 workers for three quarters.
A year ago, the factory ran on a rush and apology—late pay, last-minute overtime, and safety briefings only after an accident. The owner drew a line: finance is a servant, not the master. They posted a wage floor, cleaned up invoices, started a 13-week cash board, and told supervisors to stop work if unsafe. Then they added fair-process meetings (listen → decide → explain), a simple grievance → repair → restore path, and one-to-one congruent communications. Each Friday, managers read "we're sorry, and we fixed it" notes to close loops without blame. Five teachable SOPs (needle safety, fabric storage, overtime scheduling, client handoff, final QC) turned know-how into habit, and big decisions began with 60 seconds of quiet and a plain purpose line at the gate: *Good goods, honest work, for our neighbors.* A regional buyer responded with steadier orders. Two suppliers extended terms after six weeks of on-time, honest calls. Injuries fell, and rework dropped a third. CGTA moved from SP 1.8, SO 2.1, IN 3.2, FI 2.4 to SP 3.4, SO 3.8, IN 3.8, FI 4.8, displayed by the green area in Figure 23. The firm's posture shifted from **Jungle/Exchange** toward **Moral Sentiments**, with small, rule-bound acts of **Gratuitousness** (meal stipends on surprise shifts; mercy pricing tied to runway). The factory still watches cash closely, but the pace is steadier, the speech kinder, and promises match practice.

Result with weighted KOI and VCC averages: A movement from **cell (1,2)** (row 1 × column 2) to **cell (3,4)** (row 3 × column 4)—a strong diagonal two-cell improvement in both orientation and capacity, as shown in Figure 24. Calculations and interpretations are provided in BaM Volume 2 — Shaping a Godly Business: A BaM Monday Companion.

Figure 23. The CGT Movement of the Textile Manufacturer

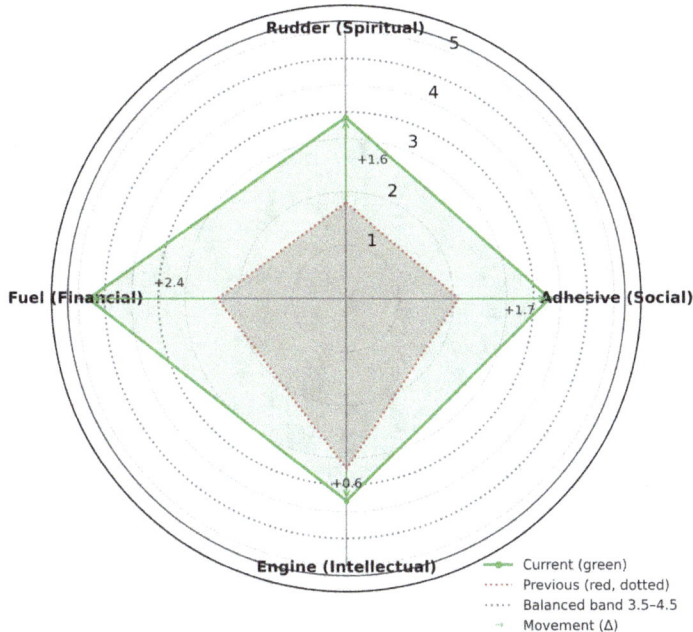

Figure 24. The Movement of the Textile Manufacturer on the 4x4 Matrix

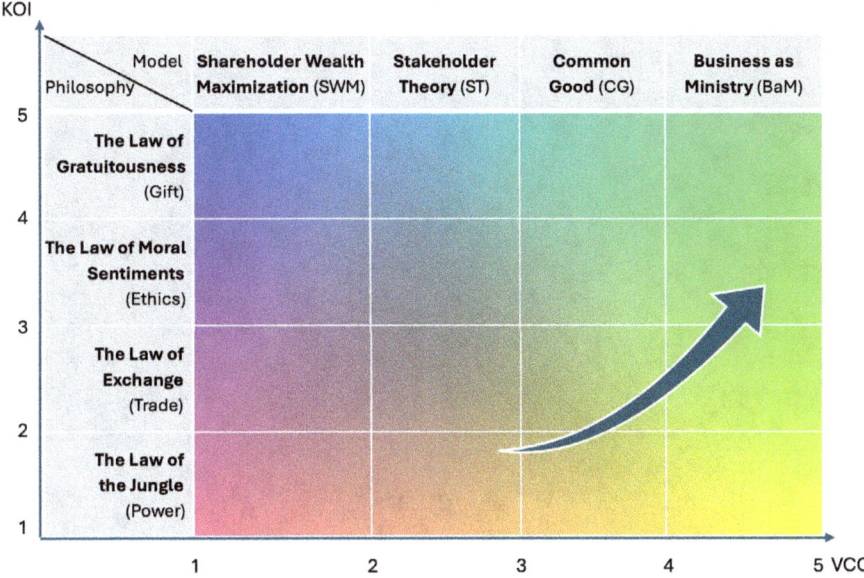

APPENDIX F. PERMISSIONS, DATA AVAILABILITY, AND PLATE CREDITS

Permissions: Figures and plates authored in this volume are released under CC BY-NC 4.0 for classroom and scholarly use with attribution. For commercial reuse, contact the publisher.

Data availability: De-identified instruments, scoring sheets, and codebooks will be posted at the publisher's website upon publication. Case data remains confidential. Excerpts provided are composites to protect participants.

Plate credits: Diagrams of the 4×4 Matrix and CGTA radar templates © 2025 by CGT Research Institute, LLC. Scripture quotations are from NIV 2011.

www.ingramcontent.com/pod-product-compliance
Lightning Source LLC
Chambersburg PA
CBHW051543230426
43669CB00015B/2708